Cambridge Elements

Elements on Women in the History of Philosophy
edited by
Jacqueline Broad
Monash University

MARY SHEPHERD

Antonia LoLordo
University of Virginia

Shaftesbury Road, Cambridge CB2 8EA, United Kingdom

One Liberty Plaza, 20th Floor, New York, NY 10006, USA

477 Williamstown Road, Port Melbourne, VIC 3207, Australia

314–321, 3rd Floor, Plot 3, Splendor Forum, Jasola District Centre, New Delhi – 110025, India

103 Penang Road, #05–06/07, Visioncrest Commercial, Singapore 238467

Cambridge University Press is part of Cambridge University Press & Assessment, a department of the University of Cambridge.

We share the University's mission to contribute to society through the pursuit of education, learning and research at the highest international levels of excellence.

www.cambridge.org
Information on this title: www.cambridge.org/9781009010542

DOI: 10.1017/9781009023740

First published 2022

A catalogue record for this publication is available from the British Library.

ISBN 978-1-009-01054-2 Paperback
ISSN 2634-4645 (online)
ISSN 2634-4637 (print)

Mary Shepherd

Elements on Women in the History of Philosophy

DOI: 10.1017/9781009023740
First published online: September 2022

Antonia LoLordo
University of Virginia

Author for correspondence: Antonia LoLordo, lolordo@virginia.edu

Abstract: There has recently been a resurgence of interest in the early nineteenth-century Scottish philosopher Mary Shepherd. This Element is intended to provide an overview of Shepherd's system, including her views on the following wide range of topics: causation, induction, knowledge of the external world, matter, life, animal cognition, the relationship between mind and body, the immortality of the soul, the existence of God, miracles, and the nature of divine creation. The author also provides an overview of relevant secondary literature and argues for their own interpretation of Shepherd's metaphysics.

Keywords: Mary Shepherd, causation, necessary connection, knowledge of the external world, women in philosophy

ISBNs: 9781009010542 (PB), 9781009023740 (OC)
ISSNs: 2634-4645 (online), 2634-4637 (print)

Contents

1 Introduction

It's recently been argued that focusing on the lives of women philosophers is counterproductive if our goal is to see them *as philosophers* (Gordon-Roth & Kendrick, 2019). Fortunately, the temptation of biography is easy to resist in the case of Mary Shepherd, who did some excellent philosophy but otherwise had an unremarkable life.[1] What we need to know can be summed up very quickly. Shepherd was born into a well-off Scottish family on December 31, 1777. She was educated at home and became interested in philosophy at a young age. In her twenties, she was involved in the Edinburgh intellectual scene. At thirty she married, changed her name from Mary Primrose to Mary Shepherd, and moved to London. There, she hosted a salon,[2] published several works of philosophy, and died just after her sixty-ninth birthday.

Shepherd's work had some readership during her lifetime,[3] but it never became part of the canon and has come back into the conversation only recently.[4] Resurgence of interest in Shepherd's work derives from recent efforts to recover the work of early modern women, along with the intrinsic interest of Shepherd's system and its convergences with some work in contemporary metaphysics.[5]

Shepherd published two books, *Essay upon the Relation of Cause and Effect* (*ERCE*) (Shepherd, 1824) and *Essays on the Perception of an External Universe* (*EPEU*) (Shepherd, 1827). The first was published anonymously; the second was published under her own name and listed her on the title page as the author of the *ERCE* as well. Three of her essays appeared in periodicals: "Observations by Lady Mary Shepherd on the 'First Lines of the Human Mind,'" in *Parriana* (Shepherd, 1828a); "On the Causes of Single and Erect Vision," in *The Philosophical Magazine* and *Kaleidoscope* (Shepherd, 1828b);[6] and "Lady Mary Shepherd's Metaphysics" (LMSM) in *Fraser's Magazine* (Shepherd, 1832). The *ERCE*, the *EPEU*, and LMSM are reprinted in facsimile in

---

[1] For more biographical information, see Brandreth (1886) or McRobert (2000a).

[2] Prominent guests included Charles Babbage, the inventor of two early computers, the Difference Engine and the Analytical Engine; the poets Elizabeth Barrett Browning and Samuel Coleridge; the economists Thomas Malthus and David Ricardo; the scientist and popularizer Mary Somerville; and the philosopher William Whewell (Brandreth, 1886, 4, 188; see also Martineau, 1877, 370–371). Babbage and Whewell in particular were close friends. Some of Shepherd's correspondence with Babbage is available in (McRobert, 2002).

[3] See, for example, Blakey (1850) and Fearn (1820) for contemporary discussions of her work.

[4] Recent work on Shepherd includes Atherton (1996, 2005), Bolton (2011, 2017, 2019), Boyle (2017, 2018, 2020a, 2021), Fantl (2016), Fasko (2021), Folescu (2021), Graham (2017), Landy (2020a, 2020b), LoLordo (2019, 2020), McRobert (1999), Paoletti (2011b), Rickless (2018), Tanner (2022), and Wilson (forthcoming).

[5] See Fantl (2016) and Wilson (forthcoming).

[6] This essay is an expanded version of the final essay in the *EPEU*.

McRobert (2000b). McRobert (2000b) also contains two anonymous 1819 works, *Enquiry Respecting the Relation of Cause and Effect* and *A Theory of the Earth*, which she attributes to Shepherd. However, Boyle (2020b) makes a convincing case against Shepherd's authorship of these works.[7] In addition, Boyle (2018) contains selections from all of Shepherd's works, arranged thematically. Complete versions of the *EPEU* and LMSM can be found in LoLordo (2020), and Garrett (forthcoming a) will include the *ERCE* and the other short pieces.

The *Essay upon the Relation of Cause and Effect*, which was written in response to an ongoing debate concerning Hume's theory of causation,[8] puts forward an original metaphysics and epistemology of causation. It is intended to show that we really do know much of what we ordinarily take ourselves to know. For instance, we really do know that everything that begins to exist has a cause, that like objects have like qualities, and that like causes have like effects.

Shepherd's goal in the *ERCE* is to explain how we acquire such knowledge. Her defense of human knowledge in this book is aimed primarily at Humeans, and she asserts that her anti-Humean conclusions "are the only true foundations of scientific research, of practical knowledge, and of belief in a creating and presiding Deity" (*ERCE* 194). In other words, Shepherd claims that her theory of causation is the only one that can serve the needs of science, everyday life, and religion. However, as we'll see in Section 5.3, Shepherd's theological conclusions are not quite as orthodox as her rhetoric might initially suggest.

I discuss Shepherd's theory of causation and some of its implications in Section 2, starting in Section 2.1 with the principle that everything that begins to exist must have a cause. In Section 2.2, I consider two implications of this principle: that cause and effect are simultaneous, and that all causation is the union of multiple objects. In Section 2.3, I examine Shepherd's second main principle of causation, that like causes must have like effects. In Section 2.4, I look at Shepherd's claim that mathematics, like physics, depends on the principle that like causes have like effects. In fact, she argues, mathematics properly understood is a branch of physics – and both concern necessary truths.

[7] Jennifer McRobert also suggests that the anonymous 1857 *Philosophy of Theism* is by Shepherd (McRobert, unpublished), but to my knowledge no other scholar has endorsed this.

[8] Shepherd refers to "a dispute which nearly lost the mathematical chair in one of our universities to the present possessor of it" (*ERCE* 5). She is referring to John Leslie, who endorsed Hume's theory of causation in passing in his *An Experimental Inquiry Into the Nature and Propagation of Heat* (Leslie, 1804). The dispute continued with interventions from Dugald Stewart (*A Short Statement of some Important Facts relative to the late Election of a Mathematical Professor in the University of Edinburgh* (in vol. 7 of Stewart (1829)) and Thomas Brown (1806, 1835). See Paoletti (2011a) and Bow (2013) for more on the Leslie affair and subsequent debate.

Shepherd's second work, the *EPEU*, is closely related to the *ERCE*. In the Preface to the *EPEU*, she explains that "[t]he conclusions . . . deduced . . . in the former *Essay* are the instruments employed in conducting the argument in this" one (*EPEU* 29/xii), and that "the subjects of the two *Essays* are capable of being considered independently, yet of throwing a mutual light upon each other" (*EPEU* 30/xiv–xv). They are supposed to illuminate each other because Shepherd's account of knowledge of the external world relies on her theory of causation, while at the same time her account of knowledge of the external world yields an account of the nature of the external world that deepens our understanding of causation.

The *EPEU* has two parts. The first part, the *Essay on the Academical or Sceptical Philosophy, as applied by Mr. Hume to the Perception of External Existence*, is aimed at refuting Hume's claim in *Treatise* that reason cannot give rise to belief in the continued, independent existence of external objects.[9] Shepherd's attempted refutation consists in explaining how reason *can* give rise to that belief. Indeed, she explains, all cognitively normal human beings have in fact arrived at belief in a continued, external, independent world through a process of "latent" reasoning (*EPEU* 37/14). Shepherd's aim is simply to make that reasoning explicit. In so doing, she is writing in opposition not just to Hume but also to Thomas Reid and Dugald Stewart, who claimed that something like natural instinct is what gives rise to our belief in continued, external, independent objects. I discuss Shepherd's account of knowledge of the external world in Section 3.1, the associated theory of vision in Section 3.2, and her account of the limits of our knowledge of the external world in Section 3.3.

Shepherd's argument for the existence of an external world uses as a premise the principle that everything that begins to exist must have a cause. She also uses a pair of structurally similar arguments to show that God exists and to show that a continuing self, independent of its particular sensations, exists. She further claims that, just as all cognitively normal human beings use reasoning to gain knowledge of the existence of a continuing, independent, external world, they use structurally similar reasoning to gain knowledge of the existence of a continuing self.[10]

[9] See *Treatise* 1.4.2 (Hume, 2001). I cite this work by book, part, and section number, as is standard.

[10] It's interesting to note that she does *not* say that all cognitively normal human beings use similar reasoning to know that God exists. I presume this is because she recognizes the existence of atheists. However, it's an interesting question what she thinks the difference is. Does she think that the argument for the existence of God simply does not occur to everyone, while the arguments for the existence of the self and the external world do? If so, why? Alternately, does she think that the argument for the existence of God does not compel belief in the way the arguments for the existence of the self and the external world do? If so, again, why?

I discuss Shepherd's argument for knowledge of a continuing self in Section 4.1, followed by her views on the mind–body relationship (Section 4.2), animal minds and organization (Section 4.3), life after death (Section 4.4), and the individuation of minds (Section 4.5). In Section 5, I discuss Shepherd's account of religion, including her views on miracles and the laws of nature (Section 5.1), as well as the existence of God (Section 5.2) and the nature of divine creation (Section 5.3). In Section 6, I conclude by examining Shepherd's description of her metaphysics as a "modified Berkeleian theory" – a description that may initially strike readers as strange, given her opposition to idealism, but turns out to be entirely appropriate given the way in which Shepherd's metaphysics makes God the ground of the world.

Shepherd's short works pick up on themes from the *EPEU*, and my discussion of them is intertwined with discussion of those themes. In "On the Causes of Single and Erect Vision" (Shepherd, 1828c), Shepherd attempts to answer two questions that Reid had recently discussed in the *Inquiry* (Reid, 1764). First, since we see with two eyes at once, why don't we see everything double? Second, since objects are "painted" upside down on the retina, why don't we see everything upside down?

Another 1828 piece, "Observations by Lady Mary Shepherd on the 'First Lines of the Human Mind'" (Shepherd, 1828a), seems to have been in some sense accidental. Shepherd had written a set of brief remarks on the philosopher John Fearn's *First Lines of the Human Mind* (Fearn, 1820). She says that these remarks were intended as a private communication. Nevertheless, Fearn had them published, along with his reply.

The last piece Shepherd published, "Lady Mary Shepherd's Metaphysics," is a continuation of her debate with John Fearn. It contains a detailed critique of Fearn's views. In addition, it also contains a short overview of her own metaphysics. This overview adds significantly to the *EPEU*, in two ways: it develops the contrast between sentient and insentient nature significantly, and it expands upon the *EPEU*'s brief remarks on unperceived motion and makes them central to the account of matter. Thus, LMSM is crucial for understanding the nature of Shepherd's materialism. Both Shepherd's account of unperceived motion and the differences between LMSM and Shepherd's earlier works deserve further attention in the secondary literature.

2 Causation

Shepherd's views on causation are striking and original. They are the first part of her system that most readers come across. As Wilson (forthcoming) shows, they resonate with contemporary discussions of causation in interesting ways. They play a foundational role in her system. And, because they are framed as a reply to Hume's inductive skepticism, they are very easy to integrate into existing courses in early modern philosophy. Perhaps for these reasons, Shepherd's views on causation have received far more attention in the secondary literature than any other aspect of her philosophy.

Shepherd's arguments about causation, induction, and necessary connection rely on two principles that have been given the following names in the secondary literature:

> The Causal Principle: every thing that begins to exist must have a cause.

For instance, "*there is no object which begins to exist, but must owe its existence to some cause*" (*ERCE* 36); "*it is a contradiction to suppose things to* BEGIN *of themselves*" (*EPEU* 100/170).

> The Causal Likeness Principle: like causes must have like effects.

For instance, "like Causes, must generate like Effects" (*ERCE* 194); "*Like effects* must have *like causes*" (*EPEU* 71/99). In both principles, the "must" is the must of metaphysical necessity.[11]

Shepherd insists that both principles can be known on the basis of reason, and indeed that all cognitively normal human beings actually do know them on the basis of reason. In arguing that the Causal Principle and the Causal Likeness Principle are known by reason, she is fighting a war on two different fronts. On one hand, she's opposing Hume, who held that objects can come into existence without a cause and that belief in the Uniformity Principle – which Shepherd's Causal Likeness Principle is a version of – derives from the imagination.[12] On the other hand, she's arguing against Thomas Reid and Dugald Stewart, who held, in opposition to Hume, that similar principles are known by common sense or natural instinct.

2.1 The Causal Principle and How We Know It

The Causal Principle is supposed to play an important role in scientific reasoning as well as everyday reasoning. It is also supposed to be the foundation of our knowledge of the existence of God. This makes it crucial that we understand exactly what the Causal Principle amounts to and what is supposed to justify belief in it. Fortunately, both issues have received a great deal of attention, at least relative to the general state of Shepherd studies.

[11] In numerous places, Shepherd insists that even God cannot violate the Causal Likeness Principle. I'll discuss the implications of this claim, and its relevance for our understanding of laws of nature, in Section 2.4.

[12] Shepherd realizes that Hume only explicitly states that something can come into existence without a cause in the *Treatise*. However, she thinks that he is "tacitly" committed to this in the *Enquiry* as well, since he there denies "*every* foundation whatever, for supposing *any cause* necessary for *any effect*" (*ERCE* 19).

Shepherd insists that "reason, not fancy and 'custom', lead us to the knowledge, That everything which begins to exist must have a Cause" (*ERCE* 27). The claim that reason yields knowledge of the Causal Principle suggests that Shepherd owes us a demonstration of the Causal Principle. Her claim that she is refuting Hume also suggests that she owes us a demonstration of the Causal Principle. For if she offers no demonstration of the Causal Principle, isn't she just begging the question against Hume?

Jeremy Fantl reads Shepherd as giving a *reductio* of the Causal Principle, and there is some textual evidence for this reading. For instance, Shepherd says that

> The idea is very soon learned, *that it is a contradiction to suppose things to* BEGIN *of themselves*; for this idea is occasioned by the impression, (the observation,) that the *beginning* of every thing is but a change of that which is already in existence, and so is not the same idea, (the same quality,) as the *beginning of being*, which is independent of previous being and its changes. The two ideas are therefore *contrary* to each other; and the meanest understanding perceives them to be so, as easily as it perceives that white is not black, &c. Changes therefore require beings already in existence, of which they are the affections or qualities. (*EPEU* 100/170)

On Fantl's view, the *reductio* fails (Fantl, 2016, 98). He suggests that the argument is supposed to be bolstered by the thesis that causes and effects are synchronous, but this is difficult to accept. Shepherd tells us that the Causal Principle and the synchronicity of cause and effect are related – but the relationship she points out is that the Causal Principle implies that cause and effect are synchronous, not the other way around (*ERCE* 38).

More recently, M. Folescu has argued that Shepherd is not *trying* to provide a conclusive or demonstrative argument for the Causal Principle (Folescu, 2021; see also Bolton, 2017). Rather, Folescu argues, Shepherd is simply trying to get her readers into a position where they can see that it is self-evident, thereby returning them to the epistemic state they were in before reading Hume. Hume had argued that the Causal Principle not only fails to be self-evident, it also fails to be evident in virtue of anything else: "every demonstration, which has been produced for the necessity of a cause, is fallacious and sophistical" (*Treatise* 1.3.3.5). This argument was aimed at John Locke and Samuel Clarke, who used the necessity of a cause as a premise in their versions of the cosmological argument.[13] Shepherd defends Locke and Clarke, as part of her

[13] For Locke, see *Essay* 4.10.3 (Locke, 1979). For Clarke, see *A Demonstration of the Being and Attributes of God* §1 (Clarke, 1998, 8).

larger project of defending the cosmological argument.[14] Far from begging the question, she thinks, Locke and Clarke saw that the Causal Principle is self-evident. Denying it is "too ridiculous . . . to consider formally": "the mind of man" is "forced to look upon all things which begin to exist as *dependent* QUALITIES" (*ERCE* 37). Despite Hume, we simply cannot help believing the Causal Principle. And in addition, we are entitled to believe the Causal Principle.

Thus Folescu (2021) characterizes the Causal Principle as "basic, foundational and, more importantly, self-evident and thus justified in other ways than by demonstration" – namely, "via intuition" (Folescu, 2021, 2). Nevertheless, Folescu argues, reasoning about the Causal Principle and other self-evident truths "can help their self-evidence shine through" (Folescu, 2021, 2). Such reasoning includes "providing indirect, non-justificatory proofs; providing extrinsic reasons for adopting them (for instance, assessing their fruitfulness for expanding a science); and assessing their relations to other foundational non-provable principles" (Folescu, 2021, 2).

Some textual evidence supports reading the Causal Principle as self-evident, in the sense of being known by intuition. Shepherd says that perceptions must have a cause distinct from themselves, for "otherwise they would each in their turn 'BEGIN their own existences' . . . which . . . is . . . an intuitive contradiction" (*EPEU* 37/14). She may have something like the Lockean sense of intuition in mind here. (It's worth emphasizing that Locke is the only one of her predecessors she ever explicitly allies herself with.[15]) For Locke, "Intuition . . . is the clearest, and most certain [kind of Knowledge], that humane Frailty is capable of" (*Essay* 4.2.1; Locke, 1979).

It's helpful to see how this reading situates Shepherd in relation to Hume and Reid. How we see the dialectic here depends largely on where we think the burden of proof lies. In the face of a broad consensus that the Causal Principle or something like it is self-evident, Hume argued that any such principle requires demonstration. His argument for this relied on the Separability Principle as a premise.[16]

The Separability Principle is a key part of Hume's overarching theory of cognition. Now, as Bolton (2019) and Landy (2020a) argue, Shepherd does not accept either the Separability Principle or the larger theory of cognition it is part of.[17] Thus, she does not feel the need to engage with the details of Hume's argument against

[14] We'll see in Section 5.3 that Shepherd's version of the cosmological argument has some surprising implications, due to her unorthodox understanding of the relationship between cause and effect.

[15] LoLordo (2019, 9).

[16] That is, the principle that the "separation . . . of the idea of a cause, from that of a beginning of existence, is plainly possible for the imagination, and consequently the *actual* separation of these objects . . . implies no contradiction" (*Treatise* 1.3.3.3).

[17] Shepherd's own theory of cognition – which is presented in fragments but seems to me to constitute a systematic whole – deserves further attention in the secondary literature.

reasoned knowledge of the Causal Principle. The dialectic is best understood not as Shepherd begging the question against Hume, but as Shepherd and Hume offering two competing theories of cognition. The choice between them should be made holistically, on the grounds of empirical adequacy and explanatory success (Bolton, 2019).

This eliminates the worry that Shepherd is begging the question. It also enables us to grasp an important point about Shepherd's goals and methodology. Throughout the *ERCE* and in the early chapters of the *EPEU*, Shepherd presents her view as a point-by-point refutation of Hume. However, this presentation is misleading. Ultimately, Shepherd is not trying to engage with Hume on his own terms. Rather, she is trying to provide a better alternative – a metaphysics and epistemology that fits the way the world is and the epistemic needs of science, religion, and everyday life.

One might worry that if Shepherd understands the Causal Principle as a self-evident truth, she is very close to Reid. But Shepherd takes herself to be an *opponent* of Reid! However, Folescu (2021) makes a strong case that Shepherd simply misunderstands the status Reid assigns to the Causal Principle and other deliverances of "common sense." If so, Shepherd is in good company: most of Reid's early readers misunderstood him in precisely this way, thinking of common sense as opposed to reason rather than constitutive of it. In fact, Reid's principles of common sense, properly understood, are not merely things we cannot help believing but things we are entitled to believe, things we count as rational in virtue of believing. According to what I see as the emerging consensus, this is precisely the status Shepherd assigns to the Causal Principle.

2.2 Cause and Effect are Simultaneous and All Causation is the Union of Multiple Objects

The Causal Principle has a number of important implications. Here, I'll discuss what I see as the two most important. First, the Causal Principle is supposed to imply that all causation requires the union of multiple objects: "The junction of two or more qualities or objects is wanted to every new creation of a new quality" (*ERCE* 187). Shepherd does not explain why the Causal Principle implies that all causation requires the union of multiple objects, but one way to see how it works is by *reductio*. Assume that a single cause can bring about an effect without mixing with anything else. Then at any given moment of its existence, it should already have brought about its effect. But this is absurd, since things that exist now can be causes of later effects.

Second, the Causal Principle is supposed to imply that cause and effect are synchronous (*ERCE* 38).[18] Shepherd insists that "although an object, in order to act as a Cause, must be in Being antecedently to such action; yet when it *acts as a Cause*, its *Effects* are *synchronous with that action*" (*ERCE* 49–50). Again, a *reductio* is helpful. Assume that two objects are mixed and that the effect is held in suspense for some period of time. Why didn't the effect come into existence immediately, at the same moment the cause came into existence? There must, Shepherd thinks, be some further cause that explains why the effect came into existence when it did and not a moment later or a moment earlier.

The basic picture here is that causation is mixture. Contra Hume and his Separability Principle, cause and effect are not distinct entities. Rather, the "*union*" of two objects "is the proximate Cause of, and is *one* with the Effect" (*ERCE* 187). For instance, "the *union of Fire and Wood*" causes – in other words, constitutes – "combustion" (*ERCE* 57). The union of fire and flesh burns the child, that is, constitutes a burn (*EPEU* 160/317–318). The union of bread and digestive system nourishes us, that is, constitutes nourishment (*EPEU* 81/125).

I say that for Shepherd, cause and effect are not distinct entities. At certain points, Shepherd makes a stronger claim: "Cause and Effect . . . are but different words for the same *Essence*" (*ERCE* 57), "the proximate Cause . . . is *one* with the Effect" (*ERCE* 187). Some scholars thus read Shepherd as thinking that cause and effect are truly identical. Some evidence for this reading is provided by Shepherd's characterization of causation as multiplication: "To represent the relation of cause and effect, as, A *followed* by B is a *false* view of the matter; cause and effect might be represented rather, as A • B = C, therefore C is *included* in the *mixture* of the objects called *cause*" (*EPEU* 146/281).

However, there are also good reasons to deny that Shepherd thinks that cause and effect are identical. The claim that cause and effect are identical is stronger than Shepherd needs, and indeed so strong that it causes serious problems for Shepherd. As we'll see in Section 5.3, Shepherd thinks that God is the cause of the world. However, given her clear opposition to atheism, I think it is unlikely that she would be willing to accept the Spinozistic conclusion that God and the world are *identical*. Moreover, as we'll see in Section 4.4, Shepherd thinks that it is epistemically possible for the mind to be united with something other than an organic body to produce the conscious self. In other words, she is committed to the possibility of one and the same effect – the conscious self whose immortality we care about – having two different causes, the mixture of mind

[18] See Landy (2020a) for an account of why this does not imply that everything happens at the same time, as opponents of simultaneous causation tend to suggest.

with a persisting organic body or the mixture of mind with some other kind of body. Again, this seems to rule out any commitment to the identity of cause and effect. Instead, Shepherd must think that effects bear some slightly weaker atemporal dependence relation to their causes.

While some scholars read Shepherd as holding that cause and effect are identical, others ascribe to her a somewhat weaker view. Martha Bolton says that for Shepherd, causation is a compositional determination relation (Bolton, 2011, §2.1). Ariel Melamedoff describes it as a form of metaphysical emergence, where the base properties are the cause and the emergent properties are the effect (Melamedoff, n.d.). One could also think of causation as a kind of grounding relation. For although contemporary philosophers tend to think of grounding as constitutive as opposed to causal (Bliss & Trogdon, 2021), for Shepherd causal relations *are* constitutive. All these ways of speaking fit well with the way in which Shepherd tends to equate effects and qualities, and they all distinguish cause and effect in some way without making them into completely distinct entities.

I am not sure it's all that useful for us to pick a dependence relation from contemporary metaphysics and try to assimilate Shepherd's notion of causation to it. But these suggestions are helpful if understood as ways of emphasizing that for Shepherd, effects depend on causes and not vice versa, in the sense that effects are *less fundamental* than their causes. Although cause and effect exist at the same time, the relationship is not symmetric. The union of fire and wood explains why there's combustion, but combustion doesn't explain why there's a union of fire and wood.

2.3 The Causal Likeness Principle

Perhaps the most important implication of the Causal Principle is the Causal Likeness Principle: like causes must have like effects.[19] Shepherd argues for this principle on the grounds that if like causes did not have like effects, there would be a "difference of existence," and such "DIFFERENCES OF EXISTENCE cannot begin of themselves" (*ERCE* 49). For a "*difference* is an *Effect*, a *change of being*, an *altered existence*, an existence which *cannot* '*begin* of itself' any more than any other in Nature" (*ERCE* 48). The reasoning here might require some spelling out. Assume for the sake of *reductio* that two like causes, A and B, have unlike effects, C and D. Assume also that A is the "one whole cause" of C and B is the whole cause of D.[20] Given the Causal Principle and the claim that it

[19] Keota Fields reads this as a biconditional: like causes must have like effects, and like effects must have like causes (Fields, forthcoming). He takes this to follow from the fact that cause and effect are "one."

[20] Shepherd explains that "any *one* of the qualities or objects needful in order to the formation of another, may be termed a *Cause*" and that the "*whole* number of objects existing, which are necessary to it, may . . . be deemed *the one whole* cause" (*ERCE* 187).

applies to differences between effects, there must be a cause of the difference between effect C and effect D. But if there is a cause of the difference between effect C and effect D, then A and B cannot have been the whole cause of C and D in the first place – they were merely partial causes (*ERCE* 45–46). Shepherd makes the same point more directly as well: if the causes are the same, "they must have like effects ... because there is nothing else given that can be supposed to make a difference" (*ERCE* 56).

I read Shepherd as holding that the Causal Likeness Principle is a self-evident deliverance of reason, something that every normal human being knows.[21] This means that the Causal Principle and the Causal Likeness Principle are epistemically on a par. When Shepherd attempts to derive the Causal Likeness Principle from the Causal Principle, she is simply providing the sort of concurrent reason that might be helpful for someone who has fallen under the spell of Humeanism. Hume argued that we can conceive of like causes having unlike effects, from which he inferred that the Uniformity Principle is not a relation of ideas and cannot be known by demonstration. He also argued that we cannot know by inductive reasoning that future like causes will have like effects. Thus, he concluded that the Uniformity Principle cannot be known by reason at all. Our belief in it must be based on some other cognitive faculty, namely imagination. Of course, since Shepherd rejects Hume's Separability Principle and the theory of cognition it relies on, this reasoning has no grip on her.

Another concurrent reason for thinking that like causes must have like effects derives from considering what makes two things "like" in the first place. Shepherd thinks of like objects as objects with like causal powers.[22] (Note that on her view, even primary qualities are causal powers, as we'll see in Section 3.3.). Thus, if two objects have different effects in the same circumstances, they must have had different causal powers. But then, ipso facto, they are not "like" after all. So much for Hume's skepticism about induction!

There is some reason to read Shepherd as holding that for two causes to be like is for them to be members of the same natural kind. She doesn't use the term "natural kind," which hadn't yet been invented, but she does equate things being like with things being "the same kind of object" (*ERCE* 148/287). And most of her examples of like causes involve natural kinds: ammonia, Epsom salts (magnesium sulfate), fire, gold, holly, mercury, oak trees, roses, and water.[23]

---

[21] We'll see in Section 4.3 that even infants and animals are supposed to know the Causal Principle and the Causal Likeness Principle.

[22] It's an important question whether this is meant to apply to *all* the causal powers of an object or simply those relevant to kind membership, although I must bracket this out here.

[23] However, not all Shepherd's examples are natural kinds, and in any case, she is often just using Hume's examples – consider bread, for instance.

Moreover, Shepherd speaks of certain properties of kinds as essential. It is "part of the definition of fire to burn certain bodies, to melt others; of bread to nourish the human body; of snow to be cold, and white" (*ERCE* 55). Despite the talk of definition, she does not, in general, mean that necessary truths like "fire consumes its fuel" or "snow is cold" are analytic. She draws a clear distinction between the *"necessary connexion* . . . of a *name*, with the *qualities which it designates*" and the "*necessary connexion* of an *object*, and its further *properties*, (or effects,) viz. those which are produced by its union with another object" (*ERCE* 154–155). That tomorrow's snow will be cold is a truth of the second sort, and as such "requires *experiment to prove its truth*" (*ERCE* 157). It is – to introduce another piece of anachronistic terminology – a necessary, a posteriori truth. We need experience to learn that one instance of snow is cold. But once we know that one instance of snow is cold, we can infer that snow is cold simply by applying the Causal Likeness Principle.

At this point, the reader might fear that Shepherd's use of the Causal Likeness Principle against Hume begs the question.[24] Recall where we are in the dialectic. Hume argues that we cannot demonstrate that like causes must have like effects, or even that like causes always *will* have like effects. Shepherd replies that the demonstration is trivial: if two causes do not have like effects, they must not have been like causes after all. The worry that might arise here is that Shepherd has made it possible for us to know that like causes have like effects only at the cost of making it impossible to know whether two causes are genuinely like. For now, in order to know if two things are genuinely like, we would have to know how they will behave in all possible circumstances.

Shepherd anticipates the worry, and her response is, on my view, compelling:

> If it should be asked . . . how is it known objects are similar upon any two occasions; the "sensible qualities may be the same, and not the *secret powers, upon which the Effects depend?*" I answer, this is to *shift* the question from the examination of *like Causes supposed*, to the consideration of the *method whereby their presence may be detected*. (*ERCE* 60)

Hume's problem has both metaphysical and epistemic aspects, and Shepherd claims to have solved the metaphysical part of the problem. Moreover, although an epistemic issue remains, it is far less serious than Hume thinks. We are, of course, fallible when we try to determine whether two similar-looking objects are really alike. But this need not lead to despair. If we are trying to make sure that two apparently similar objects are really the same, we can try to work out "the *manner* of their formation," apply "an exact experiment," or use any one of a number of other techniques (*ERCE* 127–129). Detecting whether two similar-looking things

---

[24] See Ott (2011) for a version of this worry.

are genuinely like is an interesting and important issue, on Shepherd's view, but it is not one that gives any good reason for skepticism.

2.4 Mathematics, Physics, and the Necessity of the Laws of Nature

Hume distinguished the epistemology of mathematics from the epistemology of physics in the following way. Mathematics concerns relations among ideas and thus relies on reason. Physics concerns matters of fact and thus relies on custom or imagination. Stewart rejected the claim that physics relies on custom or imagination. However, he still accepted a sharp distinction between the epistemology of mathematics and the epistemology of physics – in part because he held that the truths of physics are contingent while the truths of mathematics are necessary.[25]

In contrast, Shepherd argues that mathematics and physics are continuous and must rely on the same epistemic foundations. For mathematics and physics both depend on the Causal Principle and the Causal Likeness Principle. Our certainty that a right triangle will obey the Pythagorean theorem has the same grounds as our certainty that fire consumes its fuel:

> All mathematical demonstration is built upon the notion; that where quantities, or diagrams, resemble each other, the relations which are true, with respect to one of each kind will be true with respect to *all* others of a *like* kind; only *because there is nothing else to make a difference among them*. (*ERCE* 77)

Thus Shepherd claims that physics and mathematics form "but one science – one drawn from the bosom of that nature, whose leading principle is to exert a cause for every effect" (LMSM 807). It's worth emphasizing that the one science is *physics*: Shepherd's claim is not that physics is a branch of mathematics, as Descartes thought, but that mathematics is a branch of physics. What ultimately licenses this claim is her view of causal claims as necessary truths. For if causes necessitate their effects, then, *contra* Hume, the laws of nature must be necessary as well.

To be precise, the *law* of nature must be necessary – for on Shepherd's view, there is "one only law, '*Like cause must exhibit like effect*'" (*EPEU* 149/290). What she means, I think, is that there is only one *fundamental* law, only one law in the strict sense. Almost all of Shepherd's references to Stewart are critical, but in a rare approving mention she notes that he "considers the word *law* to be only a metaphorical expression" (*EPEU* 149n14/290n).[26] She explains that she can

[25] Hume, *Enquiry* §4.1–2 (Hume, 1975), 25–26. Stewart, *Elements* 2a.4.4.3 (Stewart, 1877, 3.316–3.317).

[26] She is referring to *Elements* 2a.2.4.2 (Stewart, 1829, 3.159).

"only give it a rational meaning, by converting it into quality, property, or relation, in which senses, when general, it forms a general efficient cause" (*EPEU* 149n14/290n). Talk of laws of nature, aside from the one law that like causes have like effects, is shorthand for talk of the causal powers of various types of objects.

This helps make clear the modal status of the laws of nature. The fundamental law that like causes have like effects is a necessary truth, relevant to understanding all possible worlds. Particular laws of nature that spell out the effects of particular kinds of objects are necessary truths too, but their relevance to understanding a particular world depends on whether that world contains the relevant kind of objects. It's a necessary truth that fire consumes its fuel, but one that would not be of much interest in science or everyday life in a world without fire. Thus, even God, on Shepherd's view, could not make snow that tastes of salt. But God *can* do something that might loosely be called changing the laws of nature: he could create apparently similar objects with various different causal powers. He could, for instance, make another kind of fluffy white stuff, with very different underlying microstructure, that tastes like salt and falls from what look like clouds.

In the period in which Shepherd was writing, it was widely, indeed almost universally, assumed that the laws of nature are contingent.[27] Shepherd recognizes this and knows that her readers will be surprised to learn that the laws of nature are necessary truths. Fearing that they might reject her theory on the grounds of incompatibility with the science of the day, she argues that her account of the laws of nature is in fact compatible with contemporary science. The main focus of this attempt is Newton's famous statement that "God may vary the laws of nature, and make worlds of several sorts in several parts of the universe."[28] Shepherd holds that her view is compatible with Newton's claim because God can vary the laws of nature – create worlds with different laws of nature – by creating worlds with different kinds of objects. Indeed, Shepherd insists, this is precisely what Newton had in mind:

> Sir Isaac Newton never meant, that if gravitation (and, by parity of reasoning, every other cause) were in the given data whence Deity formed this world . . . that it could have been a different world to what it is. He was as certain that like laws determined like results in physics as much as they do in mathematics, or in algebra; but he conceived that God could withhold from, or give gravitation (as it pleased Him) to, the original "hard particles" of which he considered all things to be formed. (LMSM 219/707)

[27] For instance, Dugald Stewart explicitly invokes Newton's authority to support the contingency of the laws of nature (*Elements* 2.4.4.3 (Stewart, 1829, 2.307–2.308)).

[28] *Opticks*, Query 31 (Newton, 1979, 403–404).

The rhetorical strategy is worth noting. Whatever Newton said must be true, because he's Newton, the great hero of nineteenth-century British philosophers. Thus, Shepherd thinks, we must read Newton in such a way that his views turn out to be true. In other words, we must read Newton in such a way that his views turn out to anticipate Shepherd's.

3 The External World and How We Know It

Hume claimed that belief in the existence of continued, external, independent objects is a "fiction" produced by the imagination.[29] Reid replied that we have a "natural instinct" to believe in the existence of a continuous, external, independent world.[30] In reply to both Hume and Reid, Shepherd offers an account of the source of our belief in the external world. That belief, Shepherd argues, is based on reason, and thus our belief in the external world rises to the level of knowledge. In the course of her argument, Shepherd gives an account of the scope and limits of knowledge of the external world; a theory of vision; and a new account of the nature of matter.

3.1 Knowledge of the Existence of an External World

Shepherd argues that all normal human beings know that an external world exists. She further argues that we have arrived at this knowledge through a process of "latent reasoning" (*EPEU* 37/14) that she makes explicit as follows. New sensations – and the term "sensation" for Shepherd includes "any consciousness whatever" (*EPEU* 34/8–9) – frequently arise in our mind. Some of these sensations appear to be of external objects. Given the Causal Principle, these new sensations must have a cause. What is that cause?

The mind, of course, is a partial cause of new sensations. But, Shepherd insists, it cannot be the whole cause. Our sensations change rapidly from moment to moment, but the mind itself does not change in the same way. Thus, there must be something else that mixes with the mind to cause sensations. We know that this something else is not in the mind – it is not an item of consciousness – so it must be *outside* or *external to* the mind.

When we speak of objects being outside or external to the mind, the "ideas are negative ones" (*EPEU* 52/50): we mean only that such objects are not items of consciousness. In other words, the line of reasoning I just outlined is not supposed to show that the external world is material. It is, however, supposed to show that the external world is mind-independent, since the same

[29] *Treatise* 1.4.2.1–2; quoted by Shepherd at *EPEU* 31/1–2.
[30] *Inquiry* 6.10 (Reid, 1764, 236).

"circumstances which go to prove that there must be truly *outward* causes, for particular sensations, prove them to be independent causes of those sensations" (*EPEU* 62/76).

Moreover, the external, independent something must exist continuously, in order to explain perceptual regularities. Consider the tree I seem to see outside my window. It has a certain "*readiness ... to appear when called for* by the use of the organs of sense" (*EPEU* 38/15). That is, it disappears when I close my eyes and reappears again when I open them. This means either that the tree creates itself anew each time I open my eyes or that it exists continuously all along, even when unperceived. But nothing can begin its own existence, so the tree cannot create itself anew each time I look at it. Therefore, it must have existed continuously, all along. Rather, to be precise, something that is external to and independent of my mind must have existed continuously all along: Shepherd's argument for the existence of continuous, independent, external objects is not supposed to show that these objects are just as we perceive them. In fact, as we'll see in Section 3.3, she concludes that our knowledge of the external world is very limited.

Even so, this argument raises a number of questions. How can we be sure that the mind does not change from moment to moment? Why couldn't it bring about all its new sensations by itself, in something like Leibnizian preestablished harmony (*EPEU* 50n3/46n)? Although Shepherd mentions this possibility, she does not argue directly against it – perhaps because she thinks it's absurd, or because she's focused on opponents like Hume whose views were still considered live options. However, she could exclude it by appeal to the principle that every cause is the union of two or more things.

Moreover, we'll see in Section 4.1 that Shepherd understands the mind as the general capacity for sensation. This seems to imply that the mind is not even the *kind* of thing that could change from moment to moment. A capacity can be actualized in different ways, but the capacity itself remains the same.

How does Shepherd exclude the possibility that it is God who is the continuous, external, independent something that mixes with the mind and sense organs to produce sensations? She refers to "*some* philosophers" who "make *God create all the images at the moment they appear in every mind*," attributing the view to Malebranche in a footnote (*EPEU* 50n2/46n). Shepherd does not spend much time ruling out this possibility, for several reasons.

First, she seems to think that the Malebranchean view, like Leibnizian preestablished harmony, simply does not require refuting. After all, Malebranche and Leibniz had been dead for well over a century, and unlike

Hume their views were not currently being revived.[31] Second, Shepherd thinks that theories on which perception requires direct divine involvement would only be worth taking seriously if they were needed to demonstrate God's existence – something she thinks she can establish on other grounds (*EPEU* 119/219). (I discuss Shepherd's argument for the existence of God in Section 5.2). Finally, Shepherd offers an argument to show that there must be multiple different causes for our various sensations. This is because the differences between our various sensations must have causes, just as the sensations themselves must have causes. For this reason, Shepherd speaks of sensations as "algebraic signs" of their causes (*EPEU* 137/261). The underlying thought is that proportionally related effects must have proportionally related causes (*ERCE* 61): "the external causes of our sensations must exist among themselves in the same proportions as do the internal varieties of sensation, their effects" (*EPEU* 129/240). Thus, sensations do not tell us what their causes are like in themselves, but they do show us something about the relationships between the causes of different sensations.

Shepherd discusses this conception of sensations as algebraic signs at some length in "Lady Mary Shepherd's Metaphysics" (LMSM 212–214/703–704). Its main role is to show, on one hand, that the causes of our sensations must vary in proportion to the variations in the sensations themselves, and, on the other, that we cannot know the intrinsic nature of external objects on the basis of our sensations. I will come back to sensations as algebraic signs in Section 3.3. First, however, it will be useful to say a little bit about Shepherd's theory of vision.

3.2 Vision

Shepherd describes sense perception as a causal process with three ingredients: the mind, the sense organs, and the external object. She says that the "organs of sense and mind, being the same, a *third* set of objects is needed" (*EPEU* 38/15) and that "the proximate cause" of sensation is the union of "the unknown, unnamed circumstances in nature . . . the organs of sense, whose qualities mix with these; and . . . the living, conscious powers necessary to sensation in general" (*EPEU* 60/71–72). But although these remarks seem perfectly general, applying to all sense modalities equally, there are in fact important differences between how different sense modalities work.

---

[31] Why does Shepherd describe the view that God creates images as they appear in the mind as Malebranche's view rather than Berkeley's? One answer is that she takes Berkeley's references to ideas being "imprinted on the senses" very seriously – far more seriously, perhaps, than charity permits. See Rickless (2018, 321–322) for more on this point. See also Atherton (1996).

To see this, it's helpful to think of sense perception as a two-stage process. The two stages are almost always simultaneous, or at least virtually so, but nonetheless it will be helpful for analytical purposes to tease them apart. The first stage consists of the mixture of the external object with the sense organ, which mixture constitutes a new state of the sense organs. The second stage is the mixture of this new state of the sense organs with the mind, which mixture constitutes a new sensation. In tactile perception, the mixture of object with sense organ is unmediated and instantaneous. Thus, the external object is itself an ingredient in the mixture that is sensation. But in the case of vision, there are intermediaries between object and sense organ, and the whole process is extended through time.

Consider the following example, which Shepherd refers to both at *EPEU* 41/25 and in a later work on vision (Shepherd, 1828b, 22b–22c). The light from the sun takes roughly eight minutes to reach us. So, if I were looking up at the sky five minutes after the sun had been extinguished, everything would be just the same as it is now. Thus, Shepherd says, "the external object becomes virtually null and void immediately upon the rays of light being emitted from it" (Shepherd, 1828b, 22b). This is an extreme case: the time light takes to travel to us from a perceived object is almost never long enough to matter. Nevertheless, the extreme case shows that the external object cannot itself be an element of the mixture that constitutes vision. Only the downstream effects of the external object on the sense organs can be an element of visual sensations.

Shepherd uses this case to show, contra Reid and others,[32] that what is seen cannot be something mind independent. The sun I see cannot be the mind independent cause of my sensation, since I would continue to have the relevant sensation for eight minutes after the disappearance of the mind-independent portion of its cause.

Shepherd's work on vision has not received much attention in the secondary literature to date, despite the fact that she herself saw it as central to her project. In an 1843 letter to Robert Blakey, she explained that her essay on single and double vision is one of three essays "whose secret principle . . . you will not find in any other authors" and that "confute modern Atheism, founded, as it is, upon fallacious inferences, from Locke, Newton, Hume, and Berkeley" (Blakey, 1879). Unfortunately, she does not explain precisely *how* her work on vision confutes modern atheism, and I will not venture an explanation on her behalf.[33]

[32] In particular, John Fearn: Shepherd replies to Fearn's *First Lines on the Human Mind* (Fearn, 1820) in Shepherd (1828a). For more on Fearn, see Grandi (2011, 2015, 2018).

[33] The other two essays concern cause and effect and final causes, and she does make clear (in case it wasn't already clear) how they confute modern atheism. All she says about vision is that "The fact of single and double vision cannot be explained consistently with any theory, and as being deducible from the general laws of causation. Such a theory is null" (Blakey, 1879, 161).

In the *Inquiry*, Reid offered a new answer to an old question: Why don't we see everything twice, given that we see everything through two eyes? He answered that seeing objects singly through two eyes is either "a primary law of our constitution" or "the consequence of some more general law which is not yet discovered" (*Inquiry* 6.19). Shepherd does not like this answer any more than she liked Reid's other appeals to common sense or instinct. Instead, she offers the following explanation. Shape perception is caused by "a line of demarcation formed by the sensation of the junction of *two colors*," and the "physical impulse producing such consciousness of colouring, is an equal proportional variety upon the retina of an eye" (Shepherd, 1828b, 13a). If we are looking at the letter A through one eye, "the perception of its figure arises in the mind, from the points of distinction between the black letter and white around it" (Shepherd, 1828b, 13a). If we are looking at the letter A through both eyes,

> [E]ach point of the figure painted on each retina will yield to the mind but *one* point of conscious black against *one* point of conscious white; and not *two* points of black against *two* points of white; because there is no intervening white painted on either retina, which can yield a consciousness of the separation of the two A's to a distance from each other. (Shepherd, 1828b, 13a)

For although there is a space between our two eyes, "the colouring of this intervening space is not painted on either retina, and therefore cannot be noticed by the mind" (Shepherd, 1828b, 13b).

This account is supposed to rely on our grasping "the truth of certain metaphysical positions," including "An object cannot be in two places at the same time" and "An object cannot exist and put forth its action *where it is not*" (Shepherd, 1828b, 13a). It is not immediately obvious how these metaphysical principles are relevant. One possibility is that the two principles are supposed to imply that visible figure can only exist in the mind. This would provide a more general argument for the claim that what is seen is not a mind-independent thing, the claim initially motivated via the example of the light from the sun that takes eight minutes to reach us. Thus, views like Reid's, on which "the mind is supposed to see the very erect object, out of itself, at a distance from itself" are absurd. It is impossible that "the mind feels colour, perceives visible figure (its result) *there, where it is not*" (Shepherd, 1828b, 22b).

It's been argued that the sun example shows that Shepherd is an indirect realist.[34] I think this is a mistake. Granted, the sun case is difficult to square with a view of Shepherd as a direct realist. But indirect realism is not the only other possibility. And if indirect realism is understood as the view that we perceive

[34] By Richard Brook, in a paper at the 2022 Eastern APA.

external objects by having a mental representation of them, Shepherd cannot possibly be an indirect realist. For on her view, we do not *perceive* external objects at all. Rather, we know that they exist because we have *reasoned* that they exist: "The perception of independent, external, and continued existence," Shepherd says, is "the result of an exercise of the reasoning powers" (*EPEU* 99/168). Again, "perception of external, continually existing, independent objects, is an affair of the understanding; it is a mental vision" (*EPEU* 99/169).

3.3 The Limits of Our Knowledge of the External World

Shepherd distinguishes two sorts of objects: internal objects, which are private – that is, necessarily available to only one mind – and outward objects, which are public (*EPEU* 48/40–41). External objects are "the acting causes of nature, independent of the senses" (*EPEU* 30/xiv; see also *ERCE* 153). Internal objects are their "sensible effects … when meeting with the human senses, and determining their specific qualities upon the mind" (*EPEU* 30/xiv). It's important to see that internal objects are not just Berkeleyan ideas of sense. Rather, they essentially refer to their external causes (*EPEU* 112/197–198). An internal object is "a compound being, consisting of a certain collection of sensible qualities, 'mixed with an *idea* the result of *reasoning*' of such qualities being formed by a 'continually existing outward and independent set of as various and appropriate causes'" (*EPEU* 112/198).[35]

In other words, an internal object is a size, shape, color, and so forth, combined with the idea that these qualities are caused by something external to and independent of my mind. For "the primary qualities, *after* the impressions they make on the senses, are sensations, or ideas, or perceptions; as well as the secondary ones" (*EPEU* 112/197). Just as we can distinguish between internal objects and external objects, we can distinguish between "*perceived internal qualities* . . . and the external *aggregates of qualities* themselves, which form the *determining causes of these on the mind*" (Shepherd, 1828a, 624). For instance, we can distinguish between what I'll call internal redness and its cause, which I'll call external redness, and between internal squareness and external squareness.

Shepherd's view, then, is that internal redness and squareness are caused by external redness and squareness. Internal redness does not *resemble* external

[35] The claim that reasoning produces new ideas is a core tenet of Shepherd's theory of cognition. She explains how this happens as follows: "that our living conscious sensations, that is, those consciousnesses which . . . admit of being compared together, with the results of their comparisons as again forming a new class of sensations … are the only, the original and immediate materials of our knowledge, is the chief feature of the philosophy I would profess" (*EPEU* 122/222).

redness. Shepherd holds that "nothing can be like a *sensation*, or *idea*, or *perception,* but a *sensation, idea,* and *perception*" (*EPEU* 112/197). Rather, internal qualities like redness and squareness are "*algebraic signs*, by which we can compute and know" the qualities of external objects (*EPEU* 137/261).[36]

This shows, again, that we know the existence of external objects without perceiving them. It also shows that our knowledge of external objects is very limited. All we know is that external objects exist, that they cause our sensations, and that they stand in certain relationships to each other. We do not know their intrinsic qualities. More generally, we do not know what they are like in themselves.

We do, however – Shepherd insists – know that external objects are material. This piece of knowledge turns out to be less impressive than it sounds, because Shepherd has a very attenuated notion of matter.

One way in which Shepherd's notion of matter is attenuated derives from the way she conceives of primary qualities. A little context might be helpful here. Locke held that material objects are substances and that they have two different kinds of qualities: primary qualities, which are categorical properties and which resemble our ideas of them; and secondary qualities, which are powers and which do *not* resemble our ideas of them. Locke's views were challenged by various later philosophers, on various grounds, and by Shepherd's day the claim that primary qualities out in the world resemble representations in our minds was pretty thoroughly discredited. However, versions of the primary quality–secondary quality distinction survived, even after philosophers gave up the claim that primary qualities resemble sensations. Reid, for instance, denied that primary qualities resemble the sensations caused by them, but still maintained some sort of primary quality–secondary quality distinction. He held that shape is a categorical property, while color is a mere power.

If the properties of external objects do not resemble our sensations, how can we gain epistemic access to them? Reid and Stewart, as Shepherd reads them, made our knowledge of the properties of external objects the result of a divinely ordained (that is, brute) psychological law: they held that "sensations . . . suggested to their minds clear immediate perceptions of external objects, totally dissimilar to themselves; that mode of suggestion being inexplicable, and by the arbitrary appointment of God" (LMSM 207n/700n). Shepherd thinks this is

[36] She also uses two other analogies: perceived qualities are like "a landscape, sent from an unseen country by which we may know it" or "a language, which must be translated, before it can explain the actions of nature" (*EPEU* 137/261). See LMSM 212/703 for more on sensations as algebraic signs. Peter West points out that Shepherd owes a debt to Berkeley here. Consider *Alciphron* 7.5, where algebraic signs, like counters at a card table, are used "not for their own sake" but as "substitutes" for something else (West, forthcoming).

absurd. Why claim that primary qualities are categorical features of objects if that means you'll have to appeal to God's arbitrary intervention to explain perception? Why not just say that for an external object to be square or extended is for it to have the power to produce certain sensations in us? In fact, at least on my reading, Shepherd goes one step further. Size and shape aren't powers that belong to matter – they *are* matter. In other words, matter is a power, rather than being the thing that has powers. For matter is "*the capacity of exhibiting upon a sentient nature, the sense of solid* EXTENSION in general" (*EPEU* 130/242).

Later, in "Lady Mary Shepherd's Metaphysics," Shepherd takes the powers of external objects to interact with each other more seriously. There, she defines matter as "unperceived extended impenetrability" (LMSM 203/697) and extension as "an unperceived cause, fitted to create or produce the idea of extension on the mind, and also to be a capacity for the admission of unperceived motion" (LMSM 203/697). This represents a change in emphasis, rather than a change in view. Even in the *EPEU* Shepherd made clear that external objects have many powers beyond the power to cause sensations, describing external objects as "those masses of unknown qualities in nature, exterior to the organs of sense, whose determination of sensible qualities to the senses forms *one class of their effects*" (*EPEU* 81/127).

In defining matter as extended and impenetrable, Shepherd is picking up on a common definition of matter in her tradition. Locke, Newton, Clarke, and others saw matter as essentially extended and impenetrable. But while they all thought of matter as a substance that *has* extension and impenetrability, Shepherd, who never uses the notion of substance, seems to think that matter simply *is* extension and impenetrability.[37]

Let's stop and look at where we are. I've said that external objects and external qualities are powers for Shepherd. I've also said that Shepherd thinks that our knowledge of the external world is very limited. She says that nature, the universe, and our friends and children are "*a whole set of corresponding, but unknown, unperceived qualities*" (*EPEU* 135–136/256). She says that "we know not what extension unperceived is" (*EPEU* 97/165). And she says that "the real essences of matter and mind we know not" (*EPEU* 130/244). We are now in a position to put the view of external objects as powers together with the view of external objects as in some sense unknown.

External objects, I argue, are unknown in the sense that we have only something like a Berkeleian relative notion of them.[38] They are powers, and

[37] Here, again she is writing in opposition to Reid, who thought that it is "an absurdity, shocking to every man of common understanding" for a power to exist without being the power *of* some being or subject (Reid, 1976, *EAP* 1.3).

[38] Or perhaps a Reidian relative conception. Reidian relative conceptions of things allow us to "know not what they are in themselves, but only that they have certain properties or attributes, or

all we know is how they manifest when they are mixed with the human mind and the human sensory apparatus to produce sensations. We can reason from our sensations to the existence of external, material objects, but such reasoning does not give us access to the intrinsic or categorical qualities of external, material objects. For external, material objects have no intrinsic or categorical properties for us to know.

4 Life and Mind

Shepherd offers a definition of the mind that parallels her definition of matter as a power: the mind is "the CAPACITY or CAUSE, for *sensation in general*" (*EPEU* 93/155). She also calls the capacity for sensation in general "soul" or "spirit" (*EPEU* 157/310). Moreover, at one point, Shepherd suggests that the capacity for sensation in general is the *self*:

> [W]hat we allude to as *self*, is a continued existing capacity in nature, (unknown, unperceived,) fitted to revive when suspended in sleep, or otherwise, and to keep up during the periods of watchfulness the powers of life and consciousness, especially those which determine the union of memory with sense. (*EPEU* 92/153)

In addition, Shepherd sometimes uses the term "mind" more broadly, to include actual sensations in addition to the general capacity for sensation that underlies them. Thus, there are broad and narrow senses of the term "mind." Given this, it's best to read Shepherd as saying that the self is the mind in the broad sense (Boyle, 2020a, 108).

The self, then, is the general capacity for sensation together with its sensations. Thus, although mind in the narrow sense is "simple" (*EPEU* 37/15) – that is, it is one indivisible capacity – the self, or mind in the broad sense, is a "complicate being" (*EPEU* 93/155). I'll start with Shepherd's account of how we know the existence of the mind in the narrow sense. I'll then look at the relationship between mind and body, animal minds, and the individuation of minds. Finally, I'll turn to Shepherd's views on immortality, which are crucial given her larger philosophical goals.

4.1 Knowledge of a Continuing Mind or Self

The field of sensations changes dramatically from moment to moment. How then do we know that there is a continuing mind – a continuing capacity for sensation – that exists in addition to our sensations and causes those sensations?

certain relations to other things" (Reid, 1976, *EAP* 1.1). It's worth noting that Reid thinks "our notion of body is not direct but relative to its qualities," namely extension, solidity, and divisibility (Reid, 1976, *EAP* 1.1).

How do I know that this mind is "*exterior* to, and independent of" these sensations (*EPEU* 55/57)?

Shepherd holds that the existence of the mind in the narrow sense can be known using a variation of the reasoning that provides knowledge of the existence of the external world. We observe that new sensations arise in our minds frequently, and we know that nothing can begin its own existence. Hence these new sensations must have a cause.

The cause of a new sensation, like all causes, must be a mixture of two or more objects. One ingredient must, Shepherd argues, be a continuing mind: "because each sensation in its turn vanishes, and new changes spring up ... there must necessarily be some *continued* existence the subject matter of these changes; otherwise, *'each change would* BEGIN *of itself*'" (*EPEU* 54/56). For "as sensation is interrupted, and is an *effect*, the original cause must be uninterrupted" (*EPEU* 92/153–154).

We saw in Section 3.3 that Shepherd sees her argument for the existence of the external world as making explicit the process of "latent" reasoning that all normal human beings use to arrive at belief in the external world. In precisely the same way, she sees her argument for the existence of a continuing self as making explicit the latent reasoning that all normal human beings use to arrive at belief in a continuing self.

By insisting that belief in a continuing self derives from reason, Shepherd is again writing in opposition to a number of different opponents. As so often in the *ERCE* and *EPEU*, she is writing in opposition to Hume and his followers, who hold that belief in a continuing self is a "fallacy, generated rather by an association, than concluded from a comparison of ideas" (*EPEU* 183/373). And, again as she often does, she is writing in opposition to Reid and Stewart, who construe belief in a continuing self as an "ultimate fact, or instinctive belief" (*EPEU* 183n1/373n). Here she has an additional opponent as well, Condillac, who argued that "the notion of SELF" can "be generated from the perception of the *memory of successive scents*" (*EPEU* 49n1/42n).[39]

Although Shepherd's argument for the existence of a continuing self is structurally similar to her argument for the existence of continuing external objects, there is one important difference. External objects, as we've seen, are causes of our changing sensations. The mind is also a cause of sensations – but in addition to causing sensations it is the *subject* of those sensations. Shepherd says that "we cannot conceive of sensation existing in, and by itself" (*EPEU* 183/373). Instead, she thinks, sensations must exist in a mind or continuing

[39] Here, Shepherd tells us she is referring to the *Traité des Sensations.* She may have in mind *Traité* §1.6.1 (Condillac, 1947, 1.238).

capacity for sensation that is "the subject matter of all changing sensations" (*EPEU* 183/372).

It may be surprising that Shepherd describes a capacity as a *subject* here. But the mind is not the subject of sensations in the sense that it is the thing in which sensations inhere as properties. Rather, it is the determinable whose determinates particular sensations are – a potentiality that can be actualized in many different ways, by many different sensations.

The knowledge of the mind we're supposed to gain from this argument is quite limited. Shepherd explains that

> [T]he continuous capacity for sensation alone is mind. Its nature we cannot tell. Its essence cannot be *matter*, or the quality of solid extension simply, because *all* matter does not *feel* with the same *interferences.* If a stone be thrown from a height, it does not suffer pain; but if there be a quality so far inhering as a dormant capacity in all matter, that being placed under certain supposed conditions, and fitly interfered with, it will feel; still that continuous capacity to sensation is a being properly termed mind;—If on the contrary, it be a quality which has its own appropriate extension as ready to be interfered with by fit organs, much more does it seem to merit that appellation, as one used in contradistinction to every other kind of extension whatever:—In either case, *the organs* or qualities which excite a *variety* of sensations, are no more the one continuous being which feels, than the hands of a watch that mark the hour, form the essence of time, or than the instruments which serve to keep alive a partial flame, are of the nature of eternal heat. (*EPEU* 184/375–376)

This is a striking passage. It tells us that mind and matter are distinct, while at the same time asserting that the nature of mind is unknown. It allows for the possibility that mind is "a dormant capacity in all matter." It also allows for the possibility that the mind is extended, although its extension would not be the solid or impenetrable extension characteristic of matter.[40] Finally, by drawing an analogy between "the one continuous being which feels" and "the essence of time" or "eternal heat," it opens up important questions concerning individuation. To understand what's going on here, we need to understand a bit about the relationship between mind and body.

4.2 The Relationship between Mind and Body

Matter is "*the capacity of exhibiting upon a sentient nature, the sense of solid* EXTENSION in general" (*EPEU* 130/242). Mind is "the continuous capacity for sensation" (*EPEU* 184/375–376). Mind and body, then, are powers.

[40] For more on this somewhat mysterious possibility, see Garrett (forthcoming a).

Shepherd suggests that her view of mind and body has the great advantage of providing an alternative to both substance dualism and materialism. It provides an alternative to substance dualism because even though it makes mind and body distinct, it does not make them distinct *substances*. Rather, on Shepherd's view mind and body are distinct powers, tailored to fit each other:

> [L]et it be considered, that the qualities of body and mind are equally unknown, save that mind is a capacity or cause for sensation in general, when that capacity shall meet with some other object to draw it forth; (for in sound sleep there seems no inherent *sentiency*, though there be animation;) and body, a capacity fitted to determine the *particular* feelings, or perceptions, of extension, colour, smell, taste, &c. upon the capacity for sensation in general; then there appears no more contradiction to me that they should thus act in, and with each other, than that any one event or object in nature should take place according to the condition of its essence. (*EPEU* 157/310–311)

Mind and body are interlocking powers that jointly produce or constitute sensation. We are conscious only of our sensations, not the mixture of mind and body that is their cause. Thus, all our experience is of mind and body already mixed together as a united thing.

Shepherd thinks that this provides the basis of a second argument against dualism. Dualists hold that "in every action of the senses, the *body* acts BEFORE *the mind and* UPON *it*" (*ERCE* 174). If that's right, we should be able to isolate the distinct causal contributions of mind and body. However, Shepherd insists, this cannot be done "by physical examination" (*EPEU* 174/349). Instead, "the powers of mind are one with THE VISIBLE AFFECTIONS of matter" (*EPEU* 174/349). This allows the mind to act and gives it "a most material agency" (*ERCE* 173).

Shepherd's view of mind and body is supposed to provide an alternative to materialism as well as an alternative to substance dualism. The form of materialism it's particularly targeted at is the materialism of the contemporary philosopher and surgeon William Lawrence.[41] Lawrence was a materialist about the mind, in opposition to opponents who believed in an immaterial soul, and also a materialist about *life*, in opposition to those vitalist contemporaries "who think it impossible that the living organic structures should have vital properties without some extrinsic aid" (Lawrence, 1822, 61).[42] On Lawrence's view,

[41] See Boyle (2021) and LoLordo (forthcoming) for more on Shepherd's objections to Lawrence's materialism.

[42] Deborah Boyle identifies the particular form of vitalism as the view of Lawrence's opponent John Abernethy (Boyle, 2021, 3). Abernethy held that life is a matter of "the superaddition of some subtile and mobile substance" (Abernethy, 1814, 41). Similarly, Shepherd says that "the first cause of life . . . must be 'extraneous' to any of the bodies among which it is found" (*ERCE* 184). Boyle reads Shepherd as holding that life is a capacity that is mixed with certain material objects. Thus, life is on a par with mind – and with gravity, which Shepherd also seems to see as

life, which "includes the notions of sensation, motion, and those ordinary attributes of living beings which are obvious to common observation," "is merely the active state of the animal structure" (Lawrence, 1822, 53). This means that sensation and all other forms of thought, as well as digestion, respiration, and the like, are simply the activity of an "organization" or organic structure (Lawrence, 1822, 80–81).

Lawrence argues that the power of sensation is constantly conjoined with "certain organic structures," and varies in complexity according to their complexity (Lawrence, 1822, 68). Combined with his explicitly Humean theory of causation (Lawrence, 1822, 69–71), this implies that organization is the cause of thought. In other words, it implies that thought is simply the action of the material brain. Because of this, Shepherd's opposition to the Humean theory of causation is also opposition to Lawrence's materialism. Indeed, in the *ERCE* Shepherd tells us that her initial reason for attacking the Humean theory of causation was precisely its role in Lawrence's argument for materialism (*ERCE* 6).

In Shepherd's view, the mere fact of a constant conjunction between organization and sensation is insufficient to establish a causal relationship. Causation requires necessary connection, and Lawrence and other similar materialists do not even try to show that sensation is necessarily connected with organization. They merely try to show that they are constantly conjoined. Shepherd agrees that sensation and organization are constantly conjoined: we see that creatures with complex brains have sensations and rocks do not. She also grants that organization is "requisite as a part of the whole causes necessary towards . . . life, sensation, and action" (*EPEU* 192/394). Her objection to Lawrence is that organization is not the *whole* cause of thought. It must be mixed with some other thing to produce sensation, namely, the mind.

4.3 Animal Minds and the Role of Organization

The "latent reasoning" by which we know the necessity of a cause and the existence of an external world is performed by virtually everyone, including "peasants," children, and even infants (*EPEU* 161/319).[43] It is also, Shepherd

a capacity distinct from matter (Boyle, 2021, 11). For more on gravity, see *EPEU* 180–192/367–371; Shepherd's discussion of gravity, and of final causes more generally, would repay further investigation.

[43] Shepherd makes this point repeatedly: see, for example, *ERCE* 92, *ERCE* 121, *EPEU* 159–161/315–319, and *EPEU* 162/323. The only sensing beings who do not know these basic principles concerning causation and existence are "idiots." In fact, this seems to be true by definition for Shepherd: "Idiocy appears to be little else, than an incapacity for further perception than what resides in the immediate impressions created by the use of the five organs of sense, and the power of motion" (*EPEU* 159/314). For beings with such an incapacity cannot grasp first

argues, performed by *animals*. She says plainly that "brutes . . . reason" (*EPEU* 106/189). As a result of such reasoning, they grasp the Causal Principle and the Causal Likeness Principle (*EPEU* 148/287). They know that the external world exists, just as we do, and they can even – contra Locke – abstract (*EPEU* 150/291). This is particularly important given Shepherd's claim that the "*faculty of abstraction, is truly the origin of all science*" (*EPEU* 149/291). The explanation Shepherd offers for this is straightforward: "animal frames, contain . . . within themselves as a component part of their existence a capacity for sensation in general" (*EPEU* 193/395–396). This is the same capacity for sensation in general that we have. In other words, animals have minds, just as we do.

In Shepherd's brief remarks on animals, she does not distinguish between the cognitive capacities of different animals. It may seem relatively plausible that my dog knows that like causes have like effects and that there is a continuous, independent external world. Perhaps my dog even knows that he has a continuing mind or self. It seems far less plausible that an oyster knows all this. Manuel Fasko argues that Shepherd can ascribe different cognitive capacities to different species of animals, just as she can ascribe different cognitive capacities to different human beings even though we all have the same kind of mind (Fasko, forthcoming). His clue is Shepherd's remark that "Sentient capacities seem . . . the result of an uniform, permanent power in nature. The varieties . . . seem to depend upon variety of organization" (*EPEU* 138/264). Sensations depend upon the mixture of the general capacity for sensation with organization. Since the general capacity for sensation is the same in all human beings, differences in the "sentient" or cognitive capacities of different human beings must result from their different organizations – that is, their different bodies. And since the general capacity for sensation is the same in all animals, differences in the cognitive capacities of different species must result from their different organizations – that is, their different bodies. The cognitive capacities of dogs are more sophisticated than the cognitive capacities of oysters because dogs have more complicated organic bodies than oysters.

4.4 Life after Death

This raises a problem. Shepherd claims to be defending orthodox religious belief. But hasn't she just said that human beings are simply complex animals? How can Shepherd say that human beings have immortal souls without also committing herself to the view that *dogs* have immortal souls? And if the

principles, which are "the perceptions of the corollaries, inclusions, or necessary relations of our simple impressions" (*EPEU* 159/314). See Fasko (2021, 188–189) for more on Shepherd's view of "idiocy," including the suggestion that Shepherd, like certain of her contemporaries, may think that idiocy is the result of a deficient sensory apparatus.

differences between individual minds depend on organization, how then can Shepherd maintain the immortality of the human soul?

Shepherd seems to have struggled with these questions, and immortality is one of the rare issues on which she seems to have substantively altered her view between the *ERCE* and the *EPEU*. In the *ERCE*, Shepherd simply bit the bullet:

> [R]eligious men are fearful that their deepest hopes may fail them, in case *any* thing of *body* is wanted, in order to *thought*. Whereas religion is not concerned in this matter so much as they imagine. If immortality is man's inheritance, it is not as a natural birthright. The meanest worm must *feel* and *think* as well as man, and yet may not be immortal.—If it [i.e. immortality] is his; it is a *gift*, which the Giver has power enough to make good by ways unseen to us. (*ERCE* 174–175)

In other words, we are not naturally immortal – but God could make us immortal, in a way we cannot understand.

The *EPEU* contains a set of essays "addressed to several friends who considered some objections overlooked" in previous work (*EPEU* 159n1/314n), and one of these essays concerns immortality. There, Shepherd begins by trying to show that the death of the body does not imply the death of the soul. After all, she says, "we do not know by any experience we have, that *all* and *only*, what we mean by *nerve*, will elicit sentiency" (*EPEU* 93/156). We "know not whether in many other beings, sensation may not go on without brain" (*EPEU* 93/156). For human beings and animals in *this* life, sensation is the mixture of the continuing capacity for thought with a brain and sense organs. Perhaps in the afterlife, the continuing capacity for thought will be mixed with something else to produce sensations. Perhaps, then, we will survive the death of our bodies in something like the way a "worm" or caterpillar survives its transformation into a butterfly (*EPEU* 94/158).

Of course, all this shows is that the death of the body does not *imply* the death of the mind. It gives no positive reason for thinking that the soul is immortal. For this reason, Shepherd goes on to offer a positive argument that the soul is immortal. The argument is both very simple and very puzzling.

Here it is. The immortality of the human soul follows from "the essential eternity of all mind" (*EPEU* 186/381), and the essential eternity of all mind follows from the fact that "capacities for being must be eternal" (*EPEU* 190/390). In other words, the human mind is immortal because it is a capacity, and all capacities are eternal. Shepherd does not say explicitly why capacities for being must be eternal – she seems to think this is obvious – but the basic idea, I believe, is that a capacity or power is not even the *kind* of thing that could come into existence or go out of existence. Capacities for being can be realized or not, but for a capacity to be unrealized is not for it to cease to exist.

Let me repeat the argument: the human mind is immortal because it is a capacity, and all capacities are eternal. As the reader has no doubt noticed, this does not really help explain the sense in which we have immortal souls and dogs do not. In fact, it raises more problems than it solves. It implies that our minds exist before we are born as well as after we die; that all minds, not just human minds, are eternal; that *matter* is eternal, since matter is also a power; and hence that God did not create either mind or matter. This seems more like Spinozism than anything that Shepherd's contemporaries would have seen as orthodox theology. And it is hard to see why we should care about having this sort of "immortality."

Perhaps for these reasons, Shepherd also tries to make the case for a special, human form of immortality:

> The proper question . . . concerning the immortality of the soul, is not whether it can survive the body as a continuous existence – for it must be eternally independent of any particular set of organs in past, as in future time.—But the inquiry should be, whether when the organs which are in relation to any individual capacity, undergo the change called death, if the *continuing mental* capacity becomes simple in its aptitudes again, or whether it remain so far in an altered state by what it has gone through in the present life, that it continues as the result of that modification? (*EPEU* 185/378–379)

It's worth working through all the various unknowns here. First, what precisely is it that survives the death of my body: my individual mind, including all its sensations – that is, the self – or just the capacity for sensation? Shepherd seems to think that both options are epistemically possible. Perhaps at death my mind will be "lost in the eternal ocean of mind," that is, become a "dormant capacity," "unexcited and unconscious of existence during eternity" (*EPEU* 185/378). Or perhaps my mind will "retain its individual consciousness of personality, communicated to it by particular interferences as in man" (*EPEU* 185/378).

Second, what would retaining individual consciousness of personality amount to? Here again Shepherd thinks several different outcomes are epistemically possible. We cannot be certain whether "[m]emory of sensations" is "obliterated or retained." And we cannot be certain whether, if memory of sensations is retained, we will "go on in a state of moral amelioration" or be "absorbed amidst the properties only subservient to animal existences" (*EPEU* 185/377–378). If memory of sensations is retained, that seems like a form of personal immortality worth caring about. If memory of sensations is retained and we also go on in a state of moral amelioration, that seems like the form of personal immortality Christians typically envision.

Shepherd holds that we cannot "demonstrate" which of these possible outcomes will actually happen. She mentions a number of considerations that speak in favor of the mind continuing to be actualized (*EPEU* 186/380) and experiencing moral and intellectual improvement (*EPEU* 182/370). However, she doesn't think these considerations are anywhere near conclusive. Ultimately, Shepherd thinks, reason can tell us that the capacity for sensation will survive the death of the body – just as every capacity continues to exist even when no longer actualized – but not whether this amounts to genuine personal immortality. Reason, in other words, cannot tell us whether the self survives death.

Fortunately, Shepherd thinks, we have another source of belief in personal immortality: "the testimony of scripture in favor of the renewal of conscious memory is as a casting die, which to any man who reasons as a philosopher, must affect his judgment" (*EPEU* 187/384). As far as I know, this is the only case where Shepherd asserts that Scripture is indispensable for knowledge of anything. Given her overarching philosophical goals, it's an important case. For this reason, it's crucial for Shepherd to demonstrate the credibility of Scripture. I'll consider the demonstration she presents in Section 5.2.

4.5 Individuating Minds

First, however, I want to return to Shepherd's suggestion that individual minds may be "lost in the eternal ocean of mind" after the death of the body. It raises the question, in virtue of what were these minds different individuals in the first place? How is the general capacity for sensation that constitutes my mind different from the general capacity for sensation that constitutes your mind?

Shepherd answers that the general capacity for sensation is carved up into distinct individuals in virtue of being associated with distinct organic bodies: "let the *capacity* to feel exist in its own extraordinary essence; let such be within the given compass of any individual organization, and this substance would exist as the capacity of an individual mind" (*EPEU* 189/388).[44] This seems to apply to *all* individual minds, not just individual *human* minds. In a discussion of the formation of animals, Shepherd asks: "What then is the use of the organs? Not to yield a creation of *original powers*, but by their *separate* actions (when excited) to be enabled by their relation with surrounding appropriate qualities of matter, to divide off from the parent stock, and become separate individual living beings." (*EPEU* 192–193/395)

---

[44] Shepherd seems to mean the "within" literally: sensations inherit the spatial location of the associated organism. (This does not make them material since they are not *impenetrably* extended.) Thus it follows, for her, that minds have a spatial location: "a man – that is, his mind – may be in the West Indies, instead of in England, in which latter place I could converse with it better than in the former" (LMSM 205/699). Indeed, Shepherd holds that minds must have a spatial location: sensation "has a necessary relation to space, by requiring space in which to exist" (*EPEU* 189/386). Given that extension – that is, space – is a power rather than a categorical property for Shepherd, the claim that minds have spatial location is less surprising than it initially seems.

Organic bodies do not *produce* the capacity for sensation, but they do carve it up into individual minds. Minds, in other words, are individuated by the associated organization.

The survival of the mind after death requires some sort of postmortem embodiment for at least two reasons. First, embodiment is necessary to individuate minds. And second, since every effect is the union of two or more things, all sensations require the union of a mind with something else. The general capacity for sensation must be mixed with something else – some postmortem body – in order for sensations to occur after death. Shepherd insists that this postmortem body will not necessarily be composed of nerves and brain, although she does not tell us anything about what other form of organization might be sufficient.

Deborah Boyle (Boyle, 2020a) argues that Shepherd's account of individuation is circular. On Boyle's reading, Shepherd says, on one hand, that the boundaries of the self are determined by the spatial boundaries of the body, and, on the other hand, that the spatial boundaries of the body are determined by what is consciously sensed. Boyle's evidence for this reading is Shepherd's claim that "we consider *that as our own body,* which is within a bound, or certain limit, and is the source of *conscious* pleasure and pain" (*EPEU* 57/62).

I think we can avoid ascribing this circularity to Shepherd. The claim of *EPEU* 57/62 is important, but it occurs in the context of Shepherd's account of the external world. As I read it, it is not intended as an explanation of why my body constitutes one unified individual, distinct from the surrounding bodies. Rather, it is supposed to explain why I *take* my body to be a unified individual distinct from the surrounding bodies. If I am right, then Shepherd does not hold that the spatial boundaries of the body are determined by what is consciously sensed, and there is no circularity of the sort Boyle fears.

What then *does* make my body a unified individual, distinct from the bodies around it? For that matter, what makes a dog, a pine tree, or a table a unified individual, distinct from the things around it?[45] I have not found an account of individuation in general in Shepherd, nor do I have one to offer on her behalf. However, it is hardly surprising for a philosopher who thinks that we do not know what external objects are like in themselves to offer no account of their individuation. Indeed, it is precisely what we should expect, given Shepherd's epistemic humility.

[45] The reader might object that for Shepherd, pine trees and tables *aren't*, or at least needn't be, distinct individuals: things with minds excepted, there is no need to carve the world of powers up into distinct individuals. However, Shepherd's claim that all causation is the union of two or more previously existing things commits her to the existence of distinct individuals wherever there are causes. Hence, it commits her to the existence of distinct individuals everywhere in the material world.

5 Shepherd's Defense of Religion and Its Implications

A defense of orthodox religion is at the heart of Shepherd's system. Her attack on Hume is motivated by what she sees as the atheistical implications of Humeanism: in particular, its implications for the cosmological argument, which Shepherd sees as the only ground for "any notion of the necessity for a Great Author, Contriver, and Arranger of the Universe" (*ERCE* 14). Hume's account of causation, on Shepherd's reading, implies that "the *custom and habit of the mind*" is "*the only ground*" for belief in the Causal Principle and "consequently [the only ground] for any notion of the necessity for a great Author, Contriver, and Arranger of the universe" (*ERCE* 13–14).

I have no doubt that Shepherd is sincere in claiming that her system is a much-needed bulwark against Humeanism and atheism. At the same time, this claim is excellent marketing. If a woman can show the falsity of atheism by doing metaphysics, then it must be acceptable for her to do metaphysics. For instance, consider an anonymous contemporary review of the *EPEU*: "If further apology be needed for this feminine intrusion into the masculine realms of science," Shepherd "claims our good will and good wishes, by defending the cause we all desire to see victorious."[46]

5.1 Miracles

The importance of Shepherd's chapter on miracles in her historical context may require some explanation. Hume's argument that testimony can never justify belief in the occurrence of a miracle was widely perceived as threatening by its early readers. Miracles played a crucial role in British philosophy because the miracles recounted in the Bible were supposed to guarantee the truth of Scripture.[47] Locke, for instance – the one previous philosopher Shepherd tries to enlist in support of her own system[48] – said that miracles are "the foundation on which believers of any divine revelation must ultimately bottom their faith."[49] Thus, one prominent opponent of Hume said that "Of Miracles" "deserves to be considered as one of

---

[46] *The Monthly Review* 3.6 (1827), 280.

[47] Miracles also played an important role in dividing Protestant philosophers from their Catholic counterparts. In reply to Hume's attempt to put all alleged miracles on the same plane, Shepherd attempts to "sink into utter disgrace Hume's childish comparison of the miracles of the New Testament with those of the Abbé Paris, and others of a similar description" (*EPEU* 170/340–341).

[48] For Shepherd's alliance with Locke, see, for example, *ERCE* 114–177 and *EPEU* 34n19/9n, 82n5/129n, and 94n4/157n. Shepherd's attempts to show that Locke is on her side have something to do with the authority of Locke in early nineteenth century Britain. But they also derive from broad philosophical sympathies. Like Locke, and unlike many of her contemporaries, Shepherd emphasizes the rational source of our most important beliefs and the special dignity of human beings as rational creatures.

[49] See, for example, Locke, *Discourse on Miracles*: miracles are the "foundation on which believers of any divine revelation must ultimately bottom their faith" (Locke, 1823, 9.257).

the most dangerous attacks that have been made on our religion."[50] Shepherd agrees with this consensus about the dangers of Humeanism, stating that "miracles are wanted" in order to "establish the authority of the doctrine [contained in Scripture], which however wise, important, or useful, would not otherwise *be binding* on the consciences of men" (*EPEU* 171/343).

By the beginning of the nineteenth century, there was an entire industry devoted to refuting Hume on miracles. Many of the miracle industry's products focused on Hume's account of testimony.[51] Others focused on his definitions of miracles and laws of nature, or on how he estimated the probability of miracles.[52] Shepherd's objections to Hume touch on virtually all the standard points: the definition of a miracle, the notion of a law of nature, and the epistemology of testimony. They are particularly striking because, at first glance, Shepherd's views on causation seem to undermine belief in miracles rather than support it. She insists that "God . . . cannot work a contradiction" and infers from this that God "cannot occasion the same objects without any alteration amidst them supposed to produce dissimilar effects" (*EPEU* 149/289). God cannot make a triangle whose internal angles add up to 270°. For precisely the same reasons, God cannot make snow that tastes like salt. How then can he make a man who's been dead for three days live again?

Shepherd tells us that "several friends" who had read her work on causation worried that her theories preclude belief in miracles, perhaps for the reasons just outlined (*EPEU* 159n1/314n). To allay this concern, she wrote an extended response to "Of Miracles" that builds on the brief account of *EPEU* 88–89/145–146. In it, she insists that "a miracle . . . is ill defined by Mr. Hume" (*EPEU* 165–166/329). For Hume's definition makes miracles a *priori* impossible.[53] But, Shepherd thinks, whether a miracle has occurred ought to be an empirical question (*EPEU* 166/329).

Shepherd's reply also brings in the epistemology of testimony. Here it's useful to contrast Shepherd with Reid as well as Hume. Reid argued that God has "implanted in our natures two principles that tally with each other . . . a propensity to speak truth" and "a disposition to confide in the veracity of others."[54] Shepherd argues that the disposition to speak truth and trust others is

---

[50] See Campbell (1766, 4).

[51] For instance, consider the well-known satire, *Historic Doubts Relative to Napoleon Buonaparte*, written by Shepherd's friend Richard Whately (1827, 27). For Shepherd's friendship with Whately, see Whately (1868, 61).

[52] Shepherd's friend Charles Babbage, for instance, argued that "Hume appears to have been but very slightly acquainted with the doctrine of probabilities" (Babbage, 1989, 41). (For a record of the friendship between Babbage and Shepherd, see McRobert (unpublished, 181–192).)

[53] To be precise, Hume's definition of miracles makes a miracle impossible given his definition of a law of nature. It would also make miracles impossible given Shepherd's definition of a law of nature.

[54] See Reid (1764, ch. 24, sec. 6). Roughly the same view is found in Campbell (1766).

"a natural consequence resulting from the experience we have of the value of truth amidst the transactions of life" (*EPEU* 165/327). This fits with a larger pattern in Shepherd's work. She thinks it's not good enough to safeguard core beliefs by attributing them to common sense or natural instinct: "'*that we are incapable of thinking otherwise than we do*', can itself be no reason that we think rightly" (*EPEU* 122/223). For this reason, she attempts to defend the rational credentials of belief in the existence of the external world and the general veracity of the people around us.

The last and most important component of Shepherd's answer to Hume on miracles concerns the laws of nature. We saw in Section 2.4 that for Shepherd, the laws of nature are necessary. Even God could not make snow that tastes of salt, although he could make something that *looks* like snow but tastes like salt. Given this, if miracles are understood as violations of laws of nature, they are *a priori* impossible. Shepherd finds this conclusion unacceptable.

To avoid it, she offers an alternate definition of a miracle: a miracle "is '*an exception to nature's apparent course*'" (*EPEU* 168/335). This is a deliberately broad definition.[55] Its key element is the distinction between the real and apparent course of nature. On Shepherd's view, the real course of nature is, necessarily, constant. But this does not imply that nature holds no surprises for us. The *apparent* course of nature *can* be changed, and in fact, such changes are common:

> [N]ature is so far from being constant in her operations, that single cases of exception occur to otherwise invariable courses of regularly antecedent and subsequent objects: thus we not only can "*imagine*," but we experience a change in the course of nature, as far as all outward appearance and modes of detection can go. On the other hand, her *real* course, in the operation of *similar cause*, must be *necessary* and *universal*. (*EPEU* 143/274)

Changes in the apparent course of nature are common because the underlying structure of nature is extremely complex, and in typical cases we know or attend to only a few of the causally relevant factors. Objects are "considered too readily as similar" (*EPEU* 150/293) if they have similar sensible qualities. Thus, we tend to gloss over the crucial distinction between the real and apparent course of nature. We act as though our very limited experience of the world is a good guide to nature as a whole. This can lead us badly astray.

On some level, this point was widely recognized. Consider Hume's example of the Indian Prince, who, upon being told that water becomes solid at low temperature, refuses to believe something that so obviously did not conform to

[55] Note that on this definition, many – perhaps most – miracles have no religious significance. For Shepherd, religious miracles are simply those marvelous events that involve direct divine intervention (*EPEU* 129/239).

his own experience.[56] Or consider the ancestor of Hume's Indian Prince example, Locke's King of Siam, who refuses to believe that water in Holland freezes so solid that an elephant could walk across it. Like Hume, Locke seems to think that his main character has acted reasonably by rejecting testimony, despite the fact that the belief he ends up with as a result of doing so is false.[57]

Shepherd, on the other hand, is very hard on the Indian Prince, who on her view should never have doubted that water freezes. He acted unreasonably, albeit in a way that is extremely common:

> The tale of the Indian Prince, who refused to believe a natural occurrence which passed the limits of his own experience, may be told of ourselves. We deem some limited observation we make, the measure of an universal fact. We draw general conclusions from particular premises, until extended knowledge acquaints us with exceptions, and sometimes with single and most important exceptions to otherwise universal facts. (*EPEU* 166/332)

Shepherd refers to "that puerile adherence to a customary association of thought, which made the Indian Prince 'a child rather than a philosopher . . . when he *refused* to believe the first relation concerning frost'" (*EPEU* 165/328–329). The Indian Prince, in other words, goes wrong because he relies on association rather than reason.

The reference to association here is worth emphasizing. One of Shepherd's chief aims in responding to Hume is to reinstate the opposition between reason and association, and thus to disprove the claim that association is the mechanism underlying all thought.[58] On her view, the beliefs produced by association serve as a kind of a quick-and-dirty heuristic, which "our Maker has ordained for practical purposes" (*EPEU* 81/127). However, the beliefs produced by association are "monstrous when held as . . . abstract truth[s] in analytical science" (*EPEU* 81/127). Shepherd sees countering the association-based tendencies of the human mind as an important task of the philosopher. It is fortunate, from her point of view, that Hume's skepticism about miracles can be seen as deriving from his reliance on association.

[56] Hume insists that although the Indian Prince missed out on acquiring a true belief, he nevertheless "reasoned justly" when he concluded that testimony about water freezing cannot be trusted (*Enquiry* 10.10).

[57] The King of Siam appears at *Essay* 4.15.5 (Locke, 1979). For a history of the Indian Prince example, see Bitzer (1998).

[58] In arguing against associationism, Shepherd is also arguing against a group of French philosophers: Condillac and his followers Pierre Jean George Cabanis, Joseph Marie De Gérando, and Antoine-Louis-Claude Destutt de Tracy (see e.g. *EPEU* 73n9/105n, 159n2/316n, etc.).

5.2 The Existence of God

Shepherd provides two complementary arguments for the existence of God (Boyle, 2018, 16). The first is the one that's supposed to be parallel to her argument for the existence of external objects (*EPEU* 90/151). It's a version of the cosmological argument:[59]

> [I]n order to account for the facts we perceive, "there must needs be" one continuous existence, one uninterrupted essentially existing cause, one intelligent being, "ever ready to appear" as the renovating power for all the dependent effects, all the secondary causes beneath our view. (*EPEU* 92/151–152)

The underlying idea is that it's "a contradiction" to suppose that God does not exist. For to imagine the nonexistence of God would be "to imagine the existence of a series of dependent effects without a continuous being of which they are the qualities" (*EPEU* 191/391). This is "equal to the supposition of the possibility of everything springing up as we see it, from an absolute blank and nonentity of existence" (*EPEU* 191/391).[60] In other words, to suppose that God does not exist is to suppose a violation of the Causal Principle. Therefore, God must exist.[61]

Shepherd conjoins this argument with a version of the argument from design: "since we perceive instruments in existence which are means to ends, there must be the director of motion, the *perceiver of ends*, the former of instruments in the universe" (*EPEU* 190/390). From this it is supposed to follow that God is a mind.

Here, Shepherd is writing in response to a contemporary materialist objection to theism.[62] The objection is that there is simply no need to posit the existence of God as designer of the universe: there are physical causes sufficient to explain the existence of each individual thing in the universe. Shepherd's response to this materialist objection is that the materialists "overlook ONE EFFECT which they

[59] See also Lascano (2019, 42–46).

[60] Shepherd's description of things in the world as "dependent effects" might seem worrying: isn't she begging the question by using as a premise that finite things are dependent? However, all she really needs is that finite things are things that begin to exist. Given the Causal Principle, this implies that they have causes and hence that they are dependent on those causes.

[61] If this argument works, it just shows that there must be some cause that does not itself begin to exist. How do we get from there to the notion of a personal God? Shepherd explains that for "devout minds, this notion becomes familiar and clear; and being mixed with the *sensible impressions* of goodness, wisdom, and power, begets those habitual sentiments of fear, trust, and love, which it is reasonable to perceive and to enjoy" (*EPEU* 92/151–152).

[62] One such opponent is Cabanis: Shepherd quotes from his *Rapports du physique et du moral de l'homme* (Cabanis, 1825). She may also be thinking of contemporaries like Holbach.

have to account for, namely, the *appearance* of contrivance in the universe" (*EPEU* 173/346).

In the next section, I'll show that Shepherd's version of the cosmological argument has unique implications because it involves her unique conception of causation. In contrast, her version of the teleological argument does not seem particularly original.

5.3 Divine Creation

Shepherd's religious commitments appear to be sincere. She gives two arguments for the existence of God, and by providing an argument for the Causal Principle, she reinforces the cosmological argument against Hume's attack. She attempts to defend the immortality of the soul, and when her system can establish that the soul is immortal only in the sense in which *every* capacity is "immortal," that is, exists forever, she turns to Scripture to buttress belief in personal immortality. And by attempting to justify belief in miracles in the face of Hume's critique, she attempts to buttress the epistemic authority of Scripture.

But although Shepherd's religious commitments are sincere, the theology embedded in her metaphysics is far from orthodox. Think of what's implied by saying that God is the cause of the world, given Shepherd's metaphysics of causation. Causes necessitate their effects, so God must necessitate the beginning of the world, rather than freely creating the world. Causes and effects are simultaneous, so God and the world are simultaneous, implying that God must exist in time. Although cause and effect are not identical, they are not distinct entities either, so God and the world must not be distinct entities. Finally, effects are qualities whose subject is their cause, so the world must be a quality of God.

The precise way in which Shepherd conceived of the relationship between God and the world seems to have changed between the *ERCE* and the *EPEU*. In the *ERCE*, Shepherd explains divine creation as follows:

> The union of *wisdom*, with benevolence; and of these with . . . "*power*" . . . might well occasion the "starting forth" of innumerable beings; the highest orders of which . . . might be considered as coeval and coequal with the Father "as touching the Godhead." But after this, the wise universe, with all its gradations of wonderful beings, with all its powers of life and heat, and motion, must have come out from him according to the laws with which they were endowed. And although the original undivided essence, whose qualities were equal to such creation, must be considered as antecedent to his own work; yet the *operation* of that essence must ever have been the same from all eternity; and in that point of view, the *junction* of wisdom and benevolence, with whatever "*capacities*" of that essence were efficient to their ends, must have been accompanied with their instant synchronous

> Effects;—the *formation of inferior beings*. "Let there be light," said God, "and there was light." (*ERCE* 97)

God's wisdom, benevolence, and power unite to form a cause. The first effect of that cause is a collection of "innumerable beings . . . coeval and coequal with" God. That effect in turn becomes a cause, and its effect is "the wise universe" that contains various wonderful beings, in addition to the powers of life, heat, and motion.

Next, Shepherd claims that God "must be considered as antecedent to his own work" and that God's operation "must ever have been the same from all eternity."[63] In what sense is God antecedent to his own work, if not in the temporal sense? The answer must be that God is antecedent to the world in the sense that God is logically prior to the world. This is precisely as it should be, given how I've presented the way in which cause and effect are related. As I understand it, cause and effect are not fully distinct entities, but they are not identical because causes are more fundamental than their effects. Similarly, God and the world are not fully distinct entities, but they are not identical because God is more fundamental than the world.

In the *EPEU*, Shepherd provides a new account of how God creates human beings, to go along with her new account of the immortality of the soul. She explains that God made man "by uniting a finite portion of mental power with the arrangement of that which was material," including "*organs* which might be the *means* of transfusing those qualities into minor portions of mind" (*EPEU* 194/400).[64] Compare the way "we, when we would apply the powers of heat, light, or electricity, to some circumscribed end, adapt thereunto those forms of artificial arrangement *not required by the original essences*" (*EPEU* 195/401). When we build a *camera obscura*, for instance, we do not thereby bring any new light into being. Rather, we harness the light that was already in existence in a specific way, in order to create an individual image.

Shepherd admits that this is an "imperfect illustration," but it is still suggestive. The creation of human beings cannot be creation *ex nihilo* as traditionally

---

[63] She adds that "God . . . archangel and angel; man . . . and animals; mind, and matter may be considered as having existed eternally, coming forth from him, living in him, and supported by him" (*ERCE* 98). Notice that the claim that mind and matter have existed eternally seems to be in some tension with Shepherd's version of the cosmological argument. For it's a premise in her version of the cosmological argument that finite beings are "dependent effects," things that came into being.

[64] The qualities of human bodies whose junction with mind enables finite perception are "like in kind, but not in degree" to qualities of God, which "already united and filling infinity, could stand in need of no organs to their determination" (*EPEU* 194/400). (The likeness in kind but not in degree is supposed to explain the sense in which human beings are created in God's image.) I read this as saying that divine immensity plays the same role with respect to God's mind as human bodies play with respect to our minds.

understood. It is simply the rearrangement of previously existing bits of mind and matter. Of course, these previously existing bits of mind and matter are themselves caused by God – but not in the sense in which God's creative activity is typically understood. They are effects or qualities of God, not wholly distinct from God.

The claim that all the particular entities that exist in the world are effects – that is, qualities – of God may sound like a form of monism. Indeed, in another context, Shepherd says that "all things in a strictly philosophical sense, form ONE NATURE" (*EPEU* 178/359). She also says that "an attribute of Deity . . . affords the subject matter and capacity for all changes" (*EPEU* 195/401; cf. *EPEU* 190/390). However, to the extent that Shepherd maintains a form of nonidentity between God and world (and between cause and effect more generally), her view is not quite monism.

To see how this works, let's think about the relationship between God and matter. To say that a divine attribute is the subject matter for change is not to say that God is extended, let alone material.[65] Shepherd does say that "the infinite intelligence is near for immediate communion in every place" (LMSM 206/6990). But because she defines extension as "an unperceived cause, fitted to create or produce the idea of extension on the mind, and also to be a capacity for the admission of unperceived motion" (LMSM 203/697), she can avoid making God extended. God is an unperceived cause, and one capable of producing the idea of extension on the mind. However, so long as God does not admit of unperceived motion – which presumably he does not – we need not see Shepherd's God as extended. Hence we can say that God grounds matter without saying that God is material. This allows matter to have some reality outside God's mind, while at the same time remaining a dependent being.

6 Conclusion: Shepherd's "Modified Berkeleian Theory"

Shepherd repeatedly distinguishes her view from contemporary forms of idealism.[66] And since her metaphysics includes the existence of matter, it would be odd, to say the least, to read her as an idealist.

Nevertheless, in the late "Lady Mary Shepherd's Metaphysics," she describes her metaphysics as "a modified Berkeleian theory" (LMSM 204/698). What does this mean? How can any theory that includes matter, no matter how attenuated the conception of matter involved is, be described as a kind of Berkeleian theory?

[65] Thanks to Keota Fields for pushing me on this point.

[66] See, for example, *EPEU* 46/37, 85n/136n, and 125/230. Unfortunately, she does not name the contemporary idealists she has in mind, and I'm not sure who they might be.

We have already seen several important points of agreement between Shepherd and Berkeley. Like Berkeley, Shepherd thinks that "nothing can be like a *sensation*, or *idea*, or *perception,* but a *sensation, idea,* and *perception*" (*EPEU* 112/197). Again like Berkeley, Shepherd thinks that there is nothing in the external world that resembles ideas of sense (to use Berkeley's term) or internal qualities (to use her own term). This is why Shepherd thinks that perceived size and shape are mere algebraic signs of unperceived material objects. More broadly, it is why she thinks we know only how material objects affect us, and not what they are like in themselves – and even why she characterizes matter itself as a power and not a substance or categorical feature thereof.

Another way in which Shepherd's system resembles Berkeley's is that the two philosophers are engaged in similar projects. They both articulate a metaphysics that is in large part aimed at rebutting atheism and restoring belief in God. Of course, as we've just seen, Shepherd's conception of God and his relationship to the world he created is quite far from any Christian orthodoxy. Nevertheless, like Berkeley, Shepherd makes God the underpinning essence of the world.[67]

Berkeley, of course, made God the underpinning essence of the world by getting rid of matter altogether. Shepherd does not do *that.* She thinks that matter exists. But on her view, matter is not merely *created* by God but also in some sense constituted by or grounded in God.

As should be amply clear by now, Shepherd is walking a delicate line here. On one hand, the fact that cause and effect are not really distinct is what guarantees that cause and effect are simultaneous and necessarily connected. Without this, her whole project – the reply to Hume on causation, induction, and miracles; the reply to Berkeley on knowledge of the existence of the external world; the arguments for the existence of God and the soul in opposition to the French materialists as well as Hume – would fall apart. On the other hand, she needs to keep a certain amount of daylight in between cause and effect. Otherwise, God would be identical to the world, ruling out any notion of creation and leading to a sort of Spinozism; our individual minds would be identical to the union of the general capacity for sensation with a certain organic body, making personal immortality impossible; and effects in general would be identical to their causes, thereby robbing most explanations in science and everyday life of their power. After all, if cause and effect are genuinely identical, then there can be no asymmetry between cause and effect – no sense in

[67] I owe the phrase to Patrick Connolly. I do not claim that this similarity is what was in the forefront of Shepherd's mind when she described her metaphysics as a modified Berkeleian theory.

which the effect depends upon the cause without the cause depending on the effect.

This is a delicate balance. Exactly how Shepherd thinks it works deserves further scholarly investigation. But it is what allows Shepherd to restore the centrality of God, as Berkeley did, while at the same articulating a metaphysics on which matter can enter into explanations in science, theology, and everyday life. Despite Berkeley's claims to the contrary, this was widely – indeed, almost universally – thought to be useful.

Of course, there are some costs of the way Shepherd does this, or at least some features of it that Berkeley himself would have seen as costs. For one thing, Berkeley would have seen Shepherd's rejection of direct realism as problematic, on the grounds that it re-introduces the possibility of skepticism. To this, Shepherd would reply that her metaphysics makes skepticism unappealing, albeit without demonstratively ruling out all possible forms of skepticism, and that this is precisely as it should be.[68] For another, Berkeley would have thought that Shepherd's metaphysics is unacceptable because it cuts us off from knowledge of things as they are in themselves. On Shepherd's view, however, this is an advantage, reinforcing the need for a certain degree of epistemic humility:

> [T]he mind strives, if possible, to find the very essences of things from the bare comparison of the relations of its ideas: for although we be philosophers enough to know it is impossible to do so, we are for ever endeavoring to catch at, and yet for ever disappointed at not meeting with, those essences. (LMSM 220/708)

Shepherd insists that her system takes us further towards knowledge in metaphysics than any of her predecessors' systems can. She has shown how we gain knowledge of God, the self, and the external world; dissolved the alleged problem of mind–body interaction; put scientific and everyday knowledge claims on new, firmer epistemic footing; and more. With all that done, she can "be resigned to whatever degree of ignorance [her] very nature renders inevitable" (LMSM 220/708).

[68] The one form of skepticism we can't rule out is the possibility of solipsism. Perhaps "the universe is contained in the existence of a single mind," and "would be dissolved in the dissolution of such individual" (*EPEU* 78/118). Shepherd grants that we cannot "*perfectly demonstrate* the contrary" (*EPEU* 78/118). However, she thinks, "the philosopher chooses equally with the peasant" to reject that "and never for one moment conceives, that on his death, an universal blank and non-existence will succeed" (*EPEU* 78/119).

Abbreviations

ERCE	Mary Shepherd, *Essay Upon the Relation of Cause and Effect* (1824)
EPEU	Mary Shepherd, *Essays on the Perception of an External Universe* (1827)
LMSM	Mary Shepherd, "Lady Mary Shepherd's Metaphysics" (1832)

References

Abernethy, J. (1814). *An Enquiry into the Probability and Rationality of Mr. Hunter's Theory of Life*. Longman, Hurst, Rees, Orme, and Brown.

Atherton, M. (1996). Lady Mary Shepherd's Case against George Berkeley. *British Journal for the History of Philosophy*, *4*(2), 347–366.

Atherton, M. (2005). Reading Lady Mary Shepherd. *The Harvard Review of Philosophy*, *13*(2), 73–85.

Babbage, C. (1989). *The Ninth Bridgewater Treatise: A Fragment* (2nd ed.). New York University Press.

Bitzer, L. F. (1998). The "Indian Prince" in Miracle Arguments of Hume and His Predecessors and Early Critics. *Philosophy & Rhetoric*, *31*(3), 175–230.

Blakey, R. (1850). *History of the Philosophy of Mind*. Longman, Brown, Green, and Longmans.

Blakey, R. (1879). *Memoirs of Dr. Robert Blakey: Professor of Logic and Metaphysics, Queens's College, Belfast*. Trübner.

Bliss, R., & Trogdon, K. (2021). Metaphysical Grounding. *Stanford Encyclopedia of Philosophy*, Winter ed. https://plato.stanford.edu/archives/win2021/entries/grounding/

Bolton, M. (2011). Causality and Causal Induction: The Necessitarian Theory of Lady Mary Shepherd. In K. Allen & T. Stoneham (Eds.), *Causation and Modern Philosophy* (pp. 242–261). Routledge.

Bolton, M. (2017). Mary Shepherd. *Stanford Encyclopedia of Philosophy*, Winter ed. https://plato.stanford.edu/archives/win2017/entries/mary-shepherd/

Bolton, M. (2019). Lady Mary Shepherd and David Hume on Cause and Effect. In E. O'Neill & M. P. Lascano (Eds.), *Feminist History of Philosophy: The Recovery and Evaluation of Women's Philosophical Thought* (129–152). Springer.

Bow, C. (2013). In Defence of the Scottish Enlightenment: Dugald Stewart's Role in the 1805 John Leslie Affair. *Scottish Historical Review*, *92*, 123–146.

Boyle, D. (2017). Expanding the Canon of Scottish Philosophy: The Case for Adding Lady Mary Shepherd. *Journal of Scottish Philosophy*, *15*(3), 275–293.

Boyle, D. (Ed.). (2018). *Lady Mary Shepherd: Selected Writings*. Imprint Academic.

Boyle, D. (2020a). Mary Shepherd on Mind, Soul, or Self. *Journal of the History of Philosophy*, *58*(1), 93–112.

Boyle, D. (2020b). A Mistaken Attribution to Lady Mary Shepherd. *Journal of Modern Philosophy*, *2*(1), 5.

Boyle, D. (2021). Mary Shepherd and the Meaning of "Life." *British Journal for the History of Philosophy*, *29*(2), 208–225.

Brandreth, M. E. S. (1886). *Some Family and Friendly Recollections of 70 Years*. C. Hooker.

Brown, T. (1806). *Observations on the Nature and Tendency of the Doctrine of Mr. Hume, Concerning the Relation of Cause and Effect*. Mundell.

Brown, T. (1835). *Inquiry into the Relation of Cause and Effect*. Scholars' Facsimiles & Reprints.

Cabanis, P. J. G. (1825). *Oeuvres completes de Cabanis* (Vols. 1–5). Bossange Freres.

Campbell, G. (1766). *A Dissertation on Miracles: Containing an Examination of the Principles Advanced by David Hume, Esq.; in an Essay on Miracles. By George* Campbell, *D. D. Principal of the Marischal College, and One of the Ministers, of Aberdeen* (2nd ed., with additions and corrections). Printed for A. Kincaid & J. Bell, sold by R. Baldwin, W. Johnston, & J. Caddel, at Buchanan's Head, in the Strand, London.

Clarke, S. (1998). *A Demonstration of the Being and Attributes of God and Other Writings* (E. Vailati, Ed.). Cambridge University Press.

Condillac, E. B. de. (1947). *Oeuvres Philosophiques; Texte établi et Présenté Par Georges le Roy* (G. Le Roy, Ed.). Presses universitaires de France.

Fantl, J. (2016). Mary Shepherd on Causal Necessity. *Metaphysica*, *17*(1), 87–108.

Fasko, M. (2021). Mary Shepherd's Threefold "Variety of Intellect" and its Role in Improving Education. *The Journal of Scottish Philosophy*, *19*(3), 185–201.

Fasko, M. (forthcoming). "The Animal Power to Feel" – Mary Shepherd's Understanding of Non-Human Animal Cognition. In K. Fields (Ed.), *Essays on Mary Shepherd: Causation, Mind, and Knowledge*. Oxford University Press.

Fearn, J. (1820). *First Lines of the Human Mind*. Longman, Hurst, Rees, Orme, and Brown.

Fields, K. (forthcoming). Does Shepherd Have a Bundle Theory of the Self? In K. Fields (Ed.), *Essays on Mary Shepherd: Causation, Mind, and Knowledge*. Oxford University Press.

Folescu, M. (2021). Mary Shepherd on the Role of Proofs in Our Knowledge of First Principles. *Noûs*, *2021*, 1–21.

Garrett, D. (forthcoming a). External Existence and the Rejection of Idealism in Hume and Shepherd. In K. Fields (Ed.), *Essays on Mary Shepherd: Causation, Mind, and Knowledge*. Oxford University Press.

Garrett, D. (Ed.). (forthcoming b). *Mary Shepherd's Essay Upon the Relation of Cause and Effect*. Oxford University Press.

Gordon-Roth, J., & Kendrick, N. (2019). Recovering Early Modern Women Writers: Some Tensions. *Metaphilosophy*, *50*, 268–285.

Graham, G. (2017). Identifying Scottish Philosophers: A Brief Response to Deborah Boyle. *Journal of Scottish Philosophy*, *15*(3), 295–297.

Grandi, G. B. (2011). The Extension of Color Sensations: Reid, Stewart, and Fearn. *Canadian Journal of Philosophy*, *41*(S1), 50–79.

Grandi, G. B. (2015). Providential Naturalism and Miracles: John Fearn's Critique of Scottish Philosophy. *Journal of Scottish Philosophy*, *13*(1), 75–94.

Grandi, G. B. (2018). On the Ancestry of Reid's Inquiry: Stewart, Fearn, and Reid's Early Manuscripts. In C. B. Bow (Ed.), *Common Sense in the Scottish Enlightenment* (pp. 77–106). Oxford University Press.

Hume, David. 1975. Enquiries Concerning Human Understanding and Concerning the Principles of Morals. In L. A. Selby-Bigge (Ed.), *3rd* Ed., Revised, P. H. Nidditch. Oxford: Clarendon Press.

Hume, D. (2001). *A Treatise of Human Nature* (D. F. Norton & M. J. Norton, Eds.). Oxford University Press.

Landy, D. (2020a). A Defence of Shepherd's Account of Cause and Effect as Synchronous. *Journal of Modern Philosophy*, *2*(2), 1–15.

Landy, D. (2020b). Shepherd on Hume's Argument for the Possibility of Uncaused Existence. *Journal of Modern Philosophy*, *2*(1), 13.

Lascano, M. P. (2019). Early Modern Women on the Cosmological Argument: A Case Study in Feminist History of Philosophy. In E. O'Neill & M. P. Lascano (Eds.), *Feminist History of Philosophy: The Recovery and Evaluation of Women's Philosophical Thought* (pp. 23–47). Springer Nature.

Lawrence, W. (1822). *Lectures on Physiology, Zoology, and the Natural History of Man*. Benbow.

Leslie, J. S. (1804). *An Experimental Inquiry into the Nature and Propagation of Heat* (special collections stacks). Printed for J. Mawman, sold also by Bell and Bradfute, Edinburgh.

Locke, J. (1823). *The Works of John Locke* (new ed., corrected). Printed for T. Tegg. Locke, J. (1979). *An Essay Concerning Human Understanding*. Clarendon Press.

LoLordo, A. (2019). Mary Shepherd on Causation, Induction, and Natural Kinds. *Philosophers' Imprint*, *19*(52), 1–14.

LoLordo, A. (2020). *Mary Shepherd's Essays on the Perception of an External Universe*. Oxford University Press.

LoLordo, A. (forthcoming). Mary Shepherd's Account of the Mind: Its Opponents and Implications. In K. Fields (Ed.), *Essays on Mary Shepherd: Causation, Mind, and Knowledge*. Oxford University Press.

Martineau, H. (1877). *Harriet Martineau's Autobiography*, Cambridge Library Collection: British and Irish History, 19th Century. Cambridge University Press.

McRobert, J. (2000a). Introduction. In J. McRobert (Ed.), *Philosophical Works of Lady Mary Shepherd* (p. 21). Thoemmes Press.

McRobert, J. (2000b). *Philosophical Works of Lady Mary Shepherd*. Thoemmes Press.

McRobert, J. (2002). Mary Shepherd and the University (2002). https://philpapers.org/rec/MCRMSA-2

McRobert, J. (1999). Mary Shepherd's Refutation of Idealism (1999). https://philpapers.org/rec/MCRMSR-2

Melamedoff, A. (n.d.). Mary Shepherd's Metaphysics of Emergence. https://philpapers.org/rec/MELMSM

Newton, I. (1979). *Opticks: Or, a Treatise of the Reflections, Refractions, Inflections & Colours of Light; Based on the 4th Ed., London, 1730*. Dover.

Ott, W. (2011). Review of Keith Allen and Tom Stoneham (eds.), Causation and Modern Philosophy. *Notre Dame Philosophical Reviews*. https://ndpr.nd.edu/reviews/causation-and-modern-philosophy/

Paoletti, C. (2011a). Causes as Proximate Events: Thomas Brown and the Positivist Interpretation of Hume on Causality. *Studies in History and Philosophy of Science Part A*, *42*(1), 37–44.

Paoletti, C. (2011b). Restoring Necessary Connections: Lady Mary Shepherd on Hume and the Early Nineteenth-Century Debate on Causality. *I Castelli di Yale* 11: 47–59.

Reid, T. (1764). *An Inquiry into the Human Mind: On the Principles of Common Sense. By Thomas Reid, D. D. Professor of Philosophy in King's College, Aberdeen*. Printed for A. Millar, London, and A. Kincaid & J. Bell, Edinburgh.

Reid, T. (1976). *Essays on the Active Powers of Man*. Garland.

Rickless, S. (2018). Is Shepherd's Pen Mightier Than Berkeley's Word? *British Journal for the History of Philosophy*, *26*(2), 317–330.

Shepherd, M. (1824). *Essay Upon the Relation of Cause and Effect*. T. Hookham.

Shepherd, M. (1827). *Essays on the Perception of an External Universe*. J. Botson and Palmer.

Shepherd, M. (1828a). Observations by Lady Mary Shepherd on the "First Lines of the Human Mind." *Parriana: Or Notices of the Rev. Samuel Parr, LL.D. Collected from Various Sources, Etc*, *1*, 624–627.

Shepherd, M. (1828b). On the Causes of Single and Erect Vision. *The Kaleidoscope; or, Literary and Scientific Mirror*, *9* (July 15, 3 and July 22, 22–23)

Shepherd, M. (1828c). On the Causes of Single and Erect Vision. *The Philosophical Magazine*, 405–416.

Shepherd, M. (1832). Lady Mary Shepherd's Metaphysics. *Fraser's Magazine for Town and Country*, *5*(30), 697–708.

Stewart, D. (1829). *The Works of Dugald Stewart* (Vols. 1–7). Hilliard and Brown.

Stewart, D. (1877). *The Collected Works of Dugald Stewart* (S. W. Hamilton, Ed., 2nd ed. improved, Vols. 1–7). T & T Clark.

Tanner, T. (2022). How Good was Shepherd's Response to Hume's Epistemological Challenge? *British Journal for the History of Philosophy*, *30*(1), 71–89.

West, P. (forthcoming). Shepherd's Modified Berkeleian Theory. In K. Fields (Ed.), *Essays on Mary Shepherd: Causation, Mind, and Knowledge*. Oxford University Press.

Whately, E. J. (1868). *Life and Correspondence of Richard Whately, D.D.: Late Archbishop of Dublin* (new ed). Longmans, Green.

Whately, R. (1827). *Historic Doubts Relative to Napoleon Buonaparte*. W. Baxter.

Wilson, J. (forthcoming). On Mary Shepherd's Essay Upon the Relation of Cause and Effect. In E. Schliesser (Ed.), *Neglected Classics of Philosophy, II*. Oxford University Press.

Cambridge Elements

Women in the History of Philosophy

Jacqueline Broad
Monash University

Jacqueline Broad is Associate Professor of Philosophy at Monash University, Australia. Her area of expertise is early modern philosophy, with a special focus on seventeenth- and eighteenth-century women philosophers. She is the author of *Women Philosophers of the Seventeenth Century* (CUP, 2002), *A History of Women's Political Thought in Europe, 1400–1700* (with Karen Green; CUP, 2009), and *The Philosophy of Mary Astell: An Early Modern Theory of Virtue* (OUP, 2015).

Advisory Board

About the Series

In this Cambridge Elements series, distinguished authors provide concise and structured introductions to a comprehensive range of prominent and lesser-known figures in the history of women's philosophical endeavour, from ancient times to the present day.

Cambridge Elements

Women in the History of Philosophy

Elements in the Series

Pythagorean Women
Caterina Pellò

Frances Power Cobbe
Alison Stone

Olympe de Gouges
Sandrine Bergès

Simone de Beauvoir
Karen Green

Im Yunjidang
Sungmoon Kim

Early Christian Women
Dawn LaValle Norman

Mary Shepherd
Antonia LoLordo

A full series listing is available at: www.cambridge.org/EWHP

Printed in the United States
by Baker & Taylor Publisher Services